# CUSTOMER SERVICE

Extraordinary Results at Southwest Airlines,
Charles Schwab, Lands' End,
American Express, Staples, and USAA

Also in the BusinessMasters Series:
*Innovation*

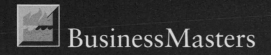
**BusinessMasters**

# CUSTOMER SERVICE

Extraordinary Results at
Southwest Airlines, Charles Schwab,
Lands' End, American Express,
Staples, and USAA

Edited by
## FRED WIERSEMA

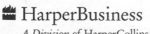 HarperBusiness
*A Division of* HarperCollins*Publishers*

HarperCollins books may be purchased for educational, business, or sales promotional use. For information please write: Special Markets Department, HarperCollins Publishers, Inc., 10 East 53rd Street, New York, NY 10022.

FIRST EDITION

*Designed by Liane F. Fuji*

Library of Congress Cataloging-in-Publication Data

   Customer service : extraordinary results at Southwest Airlines, Charles Schwab, Lands' End, American Express, Staples, and USAA / edited by Fred Wiersema. — 1st ed.
      p.  cm — (BusinessMasters)
   Includes index.
   ISBN 0-88730-772-8
   1. Customer services—Case Studies. I. Wiersema, Frederik D. (Frederik Derk) II. Series.
   HF5415.5.C844 1998
   658.8'12—dc21                           98-24870

98 99 00 01 02 ❖/RRD 10 9 8 7 6 5 4 3 2 1

# Contents

# Acknowledgments

As with the first book in the BusinessMasters series, *Innovation*, the individuals whose contributions were most important to this project were those business leaders whose insights comprise the majority of the manuscript. In sharing their experiences, goals, and visions for a corporate world where companies truly connect with their customers, the following people generously gave both time and wisdom: Steven Grant of American Express; David S. Pottruck of Charles Schwab; Michael P. Atkin, Michael J. Smith, and Ann Vesperman of Lands' End; Colleen Barrett of Southwest Airlines; Lynne Broderick, Jim Peters, Jackie Shoback, and Evan Stern of Staples; and Bill Cooney of USAA. Each highlighted company had additional people working behind the scenes, insuring that interviews went smoothly and all materials needed were on hand. Their help is also much appreciated.

At HarperCollins, Adrian Zackheim, senior vice president; Laureen Rowland, senior editor; Jodi Anderson, editorial assistant; and the rest of their team ably handled the preparation of the manuscript for publication. The talented team of editors, writers, and researchers at Wordworks, Inc., including Christina Braun, Donna Sammons Carpenter, Maurice Coyle, Erik Hansen, Susan Higgins, Susannah Ketchum, Martha Lawler, Cindy Sammons, Saul Wisnia, G. Patton Wright, and our literary agent Helen Rees have made invaluable contributions to the entire BusinessMasters series.

# Foreword

Do we really need another book on customer service? I used to believe that everything that needed to be said on this clichéd topic had already been said, and said again.

Then I read the profiles of the six extraordinary firms featured in this book, and I changed my mind.

It's not that the information in these pages is new or radical or even—here comes another cliché—cutting edge. This stuff is as rudimentary as a smile, as revolutionary as the Golden Rule. It's an eloquent reminder that companies can succeed when they base their business on doing whatever it takes to satisfy the customer. They are proof that you can make money in the process, when you realize, says Dave Pottruck of the Charles Schwab brokerage firm, that "profitability should be an outcome rather than a motive."

Every business day, the eclectic group of companies featured in *BusinessMasters: Customer Service* demonstrate a top-to-bottom, bottom-to-top commitment to customer service, starting with the bedrock belief that a great customer service culture can flourish only when front-line employees are given the unconditional support of management to do whatever it takes to satisfy the customer.

Staples, the office-supply superstore, empowers its associates "to take care of the customer at practically any cost," says president Jim Peters. This principle is echoed by Jackie Shoback, vice president of call center operations: "The philosophy that guides our work is: Let the people closest to the work make things work better." This includes a gesture as simple as allowing associates to unilaterally match a competitor's price, without making the customer jump through hoops.

Lands' End, the apparel catalog company, imposes "no limit on what an employee can offer a customer," according to Ann Vesperman, director of customer service. That takes guts! Do you—or your boss—have that kind of courage, that kind of conviction, that kind of faith in your people? Are you willing to live with the inevitable mistakes that will come when employees are empowered to do whatever it takes to please your customers? If not, you better find another way to compete, because customer service is just not going to be your thing.

I am frequently asked to give keynote speeches on customer service the Nordstrom way. Occasionally, the invitation is prefaced with the comment, "We'd like you to speak to our employees because this year we're emphasizing customer service." I am always tempted to ask, "What did you emphasize last year and what are you going to emphasize next year?"

■

Okay, so assuming you are committed to creating and supporting an entrepreneurial, customer-service environment, what kind of people do you hire?

Interestingly, most of the companies profiled in this book are not necessarily looking to hire new employees with extensive experience in their particular industry, because those people have probably already developed bad habits, such as saying "no" to the customer. At Nordstrom, managers would rather hire a nice person and teach her how to sell than hire a salesperson and teach her how to be nice. Nordstrom believes in "hiring the smile and training the skill." I once asked then-co-chairman Bruce Nordstrom who trains his salespeople, and he answered: "Their parents."

A burning desire to give great customer service "has to start in the hearts of the people who serve those clients," says Dave Pottruck of Charles Schwab. "You can train people how to do it, but I frankly believe that people are born with this interest. . . . People either like being in service to other people, or they don't."

Bill Cooney, president of the Property & Casualty Insurance Group of United Services Automobile Association, tells prospective employees, "If you don't like helping people, don't come to work here. . . . But if you do like helping people . . . this is the place to be."

Once you have those dynamic, empathetic people on your team, you must continually reinforce their positive behavior. Storytelling is a wonderful tool. Every company featured in this book recounts fabulous stories of employees performing heroic acts of customer service that were above and beyond the call of duty. These stories are the building blocks in the construction of a customer service culture because they demonstrate to new and old employees that customer service in our company is encouraged, admired, honored, and rewarded. When your employees buy into this notion and trust in management's support, they will be free to find their own creative ways to provide astonishing customer service.

If the kind of business your company is involved in is different from the companies featured in this book, don't worry about it. Customer service is customer service. It's not a strategy, but a way of life. I think Colleen Barrett of Southwest Airlines puts it best: "We are not an airline with great customer service. We are a great customer service organization that happens to be in the airline business."

ROBERT SPECTOR

# Introduction

## *The Six Masters of Service Excellence*

Bring up the topic of customer service the next time you're at a cocktail party, and you'll be bombarded with hair-raising accounts of poor treatment, stories of damage done and indignation suffered at the hands of clueless operators and apathetic associates. And pity the folks whose thankless job it is to deal with the mess when complaints start pouring in.

Broach the same subject with business colleagues, however, and more likely than not the talk will now turn to something along the lines of "Great customer service is smart business." Brace yourself for the platitudes: "Go the extra mile," "the customer is always right," "service is an investment in the future." And don't be surprised if a closer look at their companies reveals a wide gap between what is said and what is done. Like those for whom memories of poor customer experiences have grown to new heights of horror over time, those who do the manufacturing, marketing, and selling tend to elevate the virtue of their products and services.

Now talk to representatives from the six companies featured in this book—Southwest Airlines Company, Charles Schwab & Company, Lands' End, Inc., the American Express Company, Staples, Inc., and the United Services Automobile Association (USAA)—and you'll get a different take on customer service entirely, one that is neither defensive nor reactive nor apologetic. At a time when it often seems harder than ever to find a company that truly connects with its customers as individuals, these organizations are dramatic exceptions to the rule. We choose them for inclusion here because their practices transcend platitudes and lip service. Simply put, service defines their business and sets them apart from competitors.

The very managers who cite the importance of strong customer service, however, often whine about how hard it is to get employees excited about the concept. "After all," they say, "how many people do you know working in customer service who actually like it?" The people at the six companies featured here, however, are wildly enthusiastic about encouraging and maintaining a service culture: "This is our way of life," they explain. "We live this. We breathe this. We embrace this. This is it for us." And as you will see in the pages that follow, this attitude pays off.

So what's the impact? What makes these companies so different? Although they conduct their business in completely different areas of industry, these organizations actually have many things in common with regard to how they function:

**Commitment to great customer service lies at the heart**

**of their value proposition.** Customer service is the main selling point that each of these companies makes to its target customers. The first thing they want to come to mind when you think of them is, "Hey, these people are really committed to dealing with me as a customer. They provide premium service, pay attention to me as an individual, and do all those wonderful little things that everybody else seems to forget about." They turn customer service into their reason for being. In the process, they earn their customers' confidence and unwavering loyalty.

**They run a tight ship complete with well-oiled operating models.** Great customer service requires sound fundamentals. Because the basic functions at these companies are in superior shape, they don't get bogged down by the grind of cleaning up problems, correcting errors, or being on the defensive. Because their product and service defect rates are minimal, they have the luxury of turning their focus more toward pleasing customers. The saying "When you're up to your eyeballs in alligators, it's hard to drain the swamp" doesn't apply to them. Their swamps are gator-free.

**They employ the latest information technology at each level of their business.** This shouldn't be surprising: Information technology lends itself to strong customer service, and early on, these companies all recognized the advantages, the instant gratification, that the Internet and other technological advances could offer them. Rather than trying to dazzle customers with the latest bells and whistles, they use technology to make their products and services easier to acquire and operate—as well as more efficient.

These organizations stand out in three ways. First off, they use information technology to provide vastly more convenient ways for customers to interact with them. To win customers, they go beyond Ralph Waldo Emerson's adage to "make a better mousetrap [and] . . . the world will make a beaten path to [your] door." They know that building a better path to the marketplace is what truly cements customers' patronage. So they make sure there is a way callers can use their Touch-Tone phone to check on shipments, and they provide twenty-four-hour Internet access. No matter the medium, they seek to give customers the best ways possible to engage in discussion and get problems solved.

Second, they use that technology to gain a profound understanding of what these customers want and need. The notion of building profiles on every person they interact with is very important to them. If Customer A likes something different from Customer B, these companies want to know about it ahead of time. In fact, they want to know who's on the phone the moment it rings at the customer service desk. They're looking for any way they can improve efficiency while keeping customers up-to-date with the latest and greatest information.

Third, technology helps these companies track activities and processes far better than they've ever been able to track them before. They can figure out where mistakes or delays happen, then take action accordingly. This is a far better control mechanism than laying the total responsibility of tracking onto workers, and it frees up people to focus on other areas.

**Stellar customer service is a mind-set that defines the company's culture.** Customer service at each of these companies isn't relegated to a single department or function tucked away in a corner where nobody wants to deal with it. It's pervasive, it's out in the open, and it's everyone's responsibility. Whether the employee works on the front lines, in the back office, or deep within the bowels of the organization, the mind-set is the same. Customer service embodies what the company stands for. It says loud and clear: This is the way we do business.

To achieve this unity of purpose, each of the six companies has understood the importance of hiring and training the right people. Each invests heavily in thoroughly training employees, thereby enabling many of them to move from one job to another within the organization. Thus, not only do operations run smoother when emergencies arise, but also everyone has a better understanding of how the company runs—knowledge that is crucial when dealing with disgruntled customers.

**These companies build personal relationships with their customers.** They are not mass-production factories when it comes to connecting with their constituents. Each customer who deals with these organizations is given premium treatment and made to feel he or she is valued as an individual, able to call a service representative time and again. And when that customer is celebrating a birthday, has just had a child, or is mourning the loss of a family member, you can bet that the great customer service company will either acknowledge the occasion or take special action when they discover it.

This degree of one-to-one attention requires a commitment to training, to coaching, and to teaching associates the best listening strategies and most efficient methods for giving and receiving input. It takes computer technology, as well as dedicated personnel willing to record each customer interaction onto databases so it can be activated later and used as a learning tool by fellow workers.

**These organizations never stand still.** Always looking to improve, these companies are fanatical about moving forward. If there is a better way to do something, they will find it. If they have a successful product, they will seek to make it better—even if that means losing money in the short term. Never so arrogant that they refuse to learn from others, they benchmark both competitors and outside industries in pursuit of the best methods for interacting with customers.

As you will see in the chapters that follow, these companies instill these principles on an everyday basis in their dealings with customers. Representatives of each company speak for themselves in first-person accounts of the great customer service that underpins their value propositions. In listening to these individuals, you'll find that it doesn't matter whether a company is selling airplane rides, stocks, or copy paper when it comes to meeting customer needs. There is no secret potion or cosmic plan for success but rather a series of steps that at their basic level celebrate common sense and hard work. If you apply them to your own company, you can make them work for you. I've added my own thoughts and comments at the end of each chapter as a way of helping you to focus on the take-away value implicit in the lessons learned by each of these fine companies. I hope you will find them as inspiring as I have.

FRED WIERSEMA,
*September 1998*

# 1

# Southwest Airlines Company

*Luv the Customer*

*What do you call an airline that serves peanuts for breakfast, lunch, and dinner, has bunny-costumed flight attendants popping out of overhead compartments, and announces that those wishing to smoke should "file out to our lounge on the wing, where you can enjoy our feature film* Gone With the Wind*"?*

*A rip-roaring success, that's what.*

*Dallas-based Southwest Airlines Co. (www.southwest.com) has brilliantly combined a bent for wacky behavior with a reputation for stellar customer service to propel itself into the ranks of American business legend. In the process, it has grown from a three-plane intrastate start-up with only $2.1 million in annual revenues in 1971 into a $3.8 billion national player and one of the industry's most successful enterprises. The company that was originally designed on the back of a cocktail napkin now makes over 2,300 flights daily. And 1997 marked Southwest's* twenty-fifth consecutive year of profitability, as well as its sixth consecutive year of record profits.

The company has achieved its remarkable record by giving customers an inexpensive, safe airplane ride sprinkled with a lot of laughs and plenty of personal attention. Southwest's accomplishments are particularly noteworthy in an age of excess: That passengers give superb marks for customer service to an airline built on a no-frills, no-reserved-seating, no-meals approach to air travel might seem somewhat incongruous, but rave they do. So does the U.S. Department of Transportation, which for five consecutive years has acknowledged Southwest for achieving the best on-time record, finest baggage handling, and fewest customer complaints among major carriers.

What's the Southwest secret? No one would dispute that cofounder Herb Kelleher, who took over as Southwest's president and chief executive officer in 1982, is both the inspiration and the leading (funny) man for this long-running hit. But Kelleher, in turn, gives all the credit to his employees. "The hardest thing for a competitor to do is to copy our people," he says, adding that "the intangibles are more important than the tangibles." Those intangibles translate into a company esprit de corps that is second to none, prompting Fortune magazine recently to crown Southwest Airlines the best company in America to work for.

The Southwest management readily admits that employees come first, customers second, because Kelleher believes that workers who are happy are workers who take good care of customers. And, indeed, taking good care of customers is a priority. Executive vice president of customers Colleen Barrett puts it succinctly: "We are not an airline with great customer service. We are a great customer service organization that happens to be in the airline business." The company's mission statement affirms its "dedication to the highest quality of customer service delivered with a sense of warmth, friendliness, individual pride, and company spirit." Faithful adherence to this creed makes possible the airline's legendary speed (twenty-minute turnarounds versus the forty-five minutes that other airlines take), efficiency, and crowd-pleasing attitude.

That word "attitude" lies at the heart of Southwest's success, and it is nurtured by a strong corporate culture based on values and principles. There is even a Culture Committee to reinforce the attitude and make sure the airline's underdog origins aren't lost on new employees.

Far from the underdog these days, Southwest has emerged as a trendsetter, described by the Transportation Department in 1993 as "the principal driving force for changes occurring in the airline industry." Its low-fare, short-haul, no-frills style of operating forces other airlines to scramble to stay competitive wherever Southwest flies.

To keep costs low, Southwest is always on the lookout for ways to save. It flies only Boeing 737s, conformity that makes maintenance work and flight-crew training simpler, faster, and more cost-effective. It was the first airline to institute Ticketless Travel, and more than 50 percent of Southwest customers now choose that option—often purchasing seats through the company's Website.

*Then, of course, there are the nuts. Kelleher long ago had a hunch that passengers would choose low-fare tickets over so-called frills such as in-flight meals. Those who fly Southwest get a beverage and a small bag of nuts. Lest anyone forget what the modest meal represents, the bag is labeled "Frills."*

## COLLEEN BARRETT

### Executive Vice President, Customers

Value at Southwest Airlines is built on the three pillars of speed, efficiency, and customer service, just as Rollin King and Herb envisioned when they decided to start the airline. The way Herb and Rollin saw it, if you provide flights when people want to go, operate on time, offer the lowest possible fares, and make the experience enjoyable, people will fly your airline. And, boy, were they right! We now fly nearly fifty million people a year to fifty-two destinations in twenty-five states, using 262 planes on more than 2,300 daily flights.

Our "keep it simple" strategy of using short, high-frequency, point-to-point flights into less-crowded airports, combined with our no-frills approach to service, has helped keep our costs and fares low. The average length of a Southwest flight is 563 miles and costs just $72, numbers meant to compete more with ground transportation than with other airlines.

Another big factor in our success has been productivity. Although our wages are consistent with those in the rest of the industry, we seem to get a lot more effort from our workers. Because of Herb's hands-on style, we have such good labor-management relations that few people realize we are heavily unionized. Our passenger-per-employee ratio of 2,100 to 1 is about twice the average of our nearest competitor, and we need just ninety-one people to run each plane. No other major airline even comes close to getting below-hundred-person teams.

Judging by the impression Southwest workers make on passengers, though, you'd never guess there are significantly fewer of us involved in serving the public. Customer letters praise our service and often single out particular employees for their humor, creativity, and endearingly helpful ways. In our case, it really does seem that less is more.

How do we do it? The "magic" of Southwest is so simple it's almost embarrassing: We practice the Golden Rule all the time, internally and externally. Corny as it may sound, our people at every level subscribe to the notion that you should treat others the way you would like to be treated. We genuinely try to do the right thing instead of just doing things right.

Our people always come first at Southwest. I'll tell you, it really is like a family. That means we celebrate birthdays and such at work, say "thank you" often to our employees, and openly applaud those who exhibit Southwest values. One way we do that is by honoring a "Star of the Month" in our onboard *Spirit* magazine.

The January 1998 issue, for example, spotlighted Gene Fellhauer, one of our Dallas provisioning agents. Gene has been with us only two years, but he's probably touched more lives in that short span than most people do in a lifetime. He comes in early, stays late, and spends his own money to help other people. If there's a committee, he's on it. And when you ask him what makes him go out of his way for people, he'll tell you, "That's the way I was raised."

Once Gene found a diamond ring in a liquor drawer he was restocking. After correctly assuming the ring belonged to a flight attendant who had recently used the drawer, Gene tracked her down and wouldn't rest until the ring was returned. It's just that kind of behavior that we're looking for at Southwest.

As it has with Gene, we trust that the goodness of our people will pay off in spades—for each other, for customers, and, ultimately, for our stockholders. It's kind of an act of faith, but when you really treat people like family members, you have to play to people's strengths.

Part of my job is to monitor the intangibles, keep employees happy, and promote that special family feeling. I acknowledge significant events in their lives, whether they're work-related or not—births, deaths, marriages, a college graduation, whatever. I send cards and plaster the walls around here with photographs of the Southwest family. I keep Hallmark and Kodak in business!

It's gotten to be a pretty big family, though—we have close to 25,500 employees—so maintaining the personal touch is getting harder and harder. I can track some things through the computer, such as birthdays, anniversaries, and dates of hire. I comb through every status action form ever filled out on an employee, whether for a promotion, a raise, or a medical leave of absence. I also try to get payroll people in each work location to call my office with other information. The folks in payroll are usually the ones who will know when there is something significant going on in an employee's life. If there is, we want to be on top of it so that the Southwest family can be supportive.

## OUR RIVALS JUST DON'T GET IT

As Herb often says, it's the intangibles that make the difference at Southwest. Other companies have tried to copy our style, thinking they can replicate our customer service record. But it just doesn't work that way.

For more than a decade, we have had companies come and visit. They sit and they listen, but they really don't understand what we're all about. Other airlines think there's some big secret to the way we operate—the quick turns or the plastic boarding passes we use to get people on board more quickly—and they try to emulate those. But none of that is at the core of who and what we are. When you talk to people about caring for each other, treating each other decently, and finding out something personal about your employees, they look at you as if you're speaking a foreign language.

Herb had a call several years ago from the president of a very small bank. "There's something wrong with the morale of my group," he said. "I just don't know what it is. I've watched you with people, and I see how happy your folks are. Would you mind coming over one day to eat with our employees in the cafeteria and talk to them about your philosophy of life?" Herb agreed.

This executive picks Herb up and drives him to the bank. Now Herb is the most outgoing, down-to-earth human being around. He never meets a stranger. So as the two are walking into the building, Herb is speaking to all these people in the parking lot and the lobby. They ride up in the elevator, and Herb addresses everyone in the car. Along the way, he notices that the bank president doesn't speak to anybody, and it's his bank, his employees! It wasn't too hard to figure out why the morale was so low.

Some people think that you can walk up to a group of employees and say, "Okay, now you're supposed to be happy." Life doesn't work that way. It's the little things you do for people—things that show you care—that make the difference.

There probably are few people at Southwest who could not make more money elsewhere at a comparable level. Yet they don't leave. Our turnover is unbelievably low for this industry, about 7.5 percent. When you consider that we have hundreds of jobs that are on the order of entry-level ones, that's really amazing.

Executive search firms call me quite often, and I try to explain to them that money is not particularly a motivating factor for me. I want to be paid a decent salary, of course, and I want to be treated properly, but feeling satisfied and knowing that I make a difference in people's lives are more important to me than anything else. I think most of our folks feel the same: They stay here because they believe they are making a difference every day, and they feel good about what they're doing. Our lives revolve around Southwest and its culture, and that's just how we like it.

## KEEPING THE SPIRIT ALIVE

Even with our rapid expansion into different parts of the country, we've been able to transplant our culture because of the way we staff new operations. Very rarely do we open a new city with just local hires. Our unionized employees get first bid for positions at any new location, and we also hand-pick about a dozen of our very best customer service and ramp agents to go in as a team and set up the new station. But they don't just direct the physical setup; they set the tone for the camaraderie, the teamwork, we strive for everywhere. Through this process, we take a part of our culture with us each time we expand. That makes a huge difference in the success of the new operation.

The Culture Committee, which I organized several years ago, also helps to keep the Southwest spirit flourishing. Its 127 members plan celebrations, work on problems, and generally make sure that our David-and-Goliath beginnings remain a part of every employee's store of knowledge. They keep the flame alive throughout our far-flung enterprise.

Besides that, I get on my soapbox to make sure that we nurture and maintain our special identity. I meet with all classes for new flight attendants and pilots, and I visit with all our station managers at least once annually. So I'm just constantly sharing our philosophy with them and showing them examples like Gene's story. Some of our employees have used their own cars to drive customers four or five hours to a destination after a scheduling mix-up, then turn around and drive home, go to work the next morning, and not even tell us about it. We wouldn't ever know about it if the customer didn't call or write to thank us.

One young employee flew his own private plane to get someone to a hospital in time for a transplant. In more than one case, reservations agents have met customers at their destination cities and driven them to hospitals for their first cancer treatment. We have extremely caring agents, and since many people are very emotional when battling severe health problems, it's not unusual for an agent to offer assistance after learning of someone's difficulties in securing a desired flight.

I constantly get letters from customers praising agents with whom they have developed friendships just from talking on the phone. Almost every month I hear from people who tell me that after relating a hard-luck story to an employee, that employee gave up a personal incentive pass so the person could fly for free.

A skeptic might question the motives of such employees, but I can tell you that we don't ask them to do any of these things. Nor are they looking for recognition—even though we heartily celebrate such actions when we learn of them. These are just basically good people who care about other human beings. It makes me very proud, knowing these employees behave that way simply because it's the right thing to do.

## Stand by Your Men . . . and Women

We probably do a better job of empowering our people to do the right thing than most companies. We let them know that, no matter what, if they do what they think is right, the company will support them. We never criticize employees for leaning too far in the direction of the customer. A few years ago I sent a memo to station managers urging them not to use rules and regulations as a crutch when serving customers. I assured them that no employee would ever be punished for using good judgment and common sense when trying to accommodate a customer. I've never regretted that decision.

Of course, this means that customers sometimes get different levels of treatment from Southwest employees. I defend these inconsistencies: I am known, sometimes affectionately and sometimes not, as Ms. Flexibility. Flexibility allows for a lot of inconsistencies, but life doesn't always fit into nice, neat boxes. You must be willing to adapt when necessary.

Take our restricted-fare policy, for example. Like other airlines, we have a restricted fare that allows a customer to buy a flight-specific ticket at a reduced rate. Basically, it's a use-it-or-lose-it proposition. Unlike most other carriers, however, we do allow people who don't make it onto the booked flight to upgrade the ticket for another flight.

As you might expect, a hundred different things can happen to cause a traveler to want to use a restricted ticket on a flight other than the one booked—and the traveler always wants to go at the same fare. Now the rules are very clear. If you didn't enforce them, no one would ever buy a full-fare ticket again. With seventy flights a day between Dallas and Houston, for instance, why would anybody pay a regular fare? So Herb is insistent on that particular policy.

But now let's imagine that John Smith is in Houston and he's supposed to be taking a 4:00 P.M. plane back to Dallas. He gets an emergency phone call that his wife has been rushed to the hospital, so he goes to the airport and tells the ticket agent that he wants to get on the 3:00 P.M. plane instead and that he doesn't want to pay any more money. In such a situation we let the employee make the call.

Clearly, the right thing to do in this case is to put Smith on the airplane and give him as little grief as possible. But, unfortunately, not everyone tells the truth; people tell us every story imaginable to get onto a Friday-night flight that's already overbooked. So an employee has to use some judgment and some ingenuity. There are lots of different ways to check out a story without suggesting that the customer is a liar. You can just ask, for example, "Which hospital is your wife in?" Generally, based on the reaction to a question like that, you can tell whether someone is telling the truth.

Back to John Smith. Suppose the ticket agent decides Smith is telling the truth and lets him go. And then suppose that, a week later, some other fellow encounters a similar situation, knows John Smith and how we handled his case, but is arrogant and treats our agent despicably. The agent decides not to allow him to travel at the reduced rate. We may very well receive a customer complaint letter that says, "I know that your ticket agent allowed this last week for my friend, but the agent that I dealt with today didn't allow it." In this case I would write back, "I'm sorry that we disappointed you, but we do allow our people to make judgment calls. And in this particular case, the judgment call didn't go in your favor."

We come down pretty hard on employees only when they fail to use common sense. We had a situation some years back when an employee slammed the door to a jetway just as a passenger was coming down the ramp because he wanted to push the plane out on time. Now, when we say we are an on-time airline and we won't hold planes for anyone, we have to use good judgment. To make matters even worse, in this case the agent could see that the tardy passenger was wheelchair-bound and should not be made to wait four and a half hours for the next flight.

## HIRE FOR ATTITUDE

Much of the fun of flying Southwest—the jokes, the singing, the silly costumes—comes from our employees' creative personalities. We encourage them to be themselves, to be individualistic in their customer service. But that means that, occasionally, someone is going to tell a joke that is not appreciated by everyone on the airplane or sitting in the gate lounge. When that happens, you have to step up to the plate and tell customers, "We didn't handle the situation properly and we're sorry."

At the same time, however, you also have to make sure

that you don't dampen an employee's spirit. When you hire people for their personality and creativity, you don't want to inhibit them. That doesn't mean that you can't counsel them in the right way. If you're going to encourage individual decision making and creativity, you'd better have employees who know how to use their common sense and good judgment. Otherwise, you could really have a mess on your hands.

When it comes to hiring, Herb believes that attitude is a far more important attribute than education and experience. Anybody can be trained for skills, but a good attitude cannot be taught. Our hiring practices rest on the notion that humor helps people stay creative under pressure, work and play more enthusiastically, and stay healthier in the process. We look for people who have a sense of play and know when not to take themselves too seriously.

We once had a group of pilot applicants show up for interviews dressed in business suits and carrying briefcases. Kidded about their uptight appearance, they were encouraged to change into the "typical" Southwest working attire—Bermuda shorts. Six of them donned the shorts but then turned the incident into a zany kind of Southwest experience by keeping on their dark suit coats, dress shoes, and black socks. They got the jobs.

Finding the right people is easier for us than for many companies because, for the great majority of positions, we don't have to go out and recruit. We have a hundred thousand applicants for the few thousand jobs that we offer in any given year. We've been very lucky in that regard, and I think that's a real plus.

When we do recruit, we use brochures and want ads designed to attract fun-loving types who aren't afraid to "color outside the lines." Such ads have a twofold purpose: They appeal to the kind of people we're looking for, and they turn off the kind of person who wouldn't fit in here anyway.

Another important factor is that for almost all of our public-contact jobs we interview groups of thirty, forty, or fifty people in a room at one time. Although a good candidate or two may sometimes be lost, conducting group interviews means the superstars are going to pop out at you.

In these group interviews, Southwest often uses an exercise that requires people to prepare five-minute presentations about themselves. The important thing the interviewer looks for is not necessarily how well each candidate performs but how the rest of the group responds during each presentation. Applicants who enthusiastically cheer on the speakers get high marks for their unselfish and supportive attitudes. Those who look over their own notes and ignore their fellow presenters leave without jobs.

Prospective employees might also be asked to tell about a time when they used their sense of humor to get out of a sticky situation. A new one that I heard about recently required the applicants to draw themselves on a piece of paper and then stand up and explain their motivations. No matter what form it takes, the group interview process is aimed at getting people to show their true colors, their gregariousness, and enthusiasm. If you're a wallflower, you might very well be capable of providing warm service. But you're probably not going to stand out at Southwest, nor are you likely to get through the interview process.

Don't misunderstand me—we look for extroverts, not crazy people. Sometimes our quest for creativity is misconstrued. You can't imagine some of the applications that we get because people think that the crazier they are, the more likely we are to want to hire them. That is not necessarily true. There has to be the right mix: one part supportive, one part friendly, and one part zany.

## INEXPERIENCE CAN BE A PLUS

Nine times out of ten, we don't find experience at another airline to be a particular plus in hiring new people. There are some technical jobs where it is a plus, but generally we operate so differently from the norm that such prior training is of little use. Our philosophy, principles, and core values clearly contrast those found at other carriers.

When we say that we care about what our employees think and that we welcome their suggestions and complaints, we really mean it. I'm told that at most other companies—not just airlines—that way of operating is only given lip service. No one truly cares about living up to it. So if somebody has been with another carrier for eight, ten, twelve years, we're going to have to work awfully hard to change his or her mind-set. And truthfully, I find it easier to bring in an enthusiastic, brand-spanking-new person who thinks she can do everything and then mold her in the Southwest way.

Far from merely giving lip service to the notion of hearing what employees have to say, we pride ourselves on spending a lot of time listening to what they learn from being in the field. Anyone at Southwest with a manager title or higher must do at least four field visits a year in departments other than his or her own. And when I say visits, I don't mean that you go sit down with a station manager in his office and drink coffee; you really work.

I might, for instance, be stationed at a baggage check-in where I'm tagging bags and putting them on the bag belt. Or I might find myself working next to a gate agent for a day. A manager in an airport in Seattle might even travel to Dallas to work in a baggage area there. We encourage such long-distance visits because our locations vary drastically in terms of facilities and problems, and it's important to be ready for anything.

Workers also routinely cross over to train in various positions, then pitch in to help their fellow employees as needed. It's not uncommon for pilots to help flight attendants clean up as people leave the plane. Herb goes out on the busiest travel day of the year—the "Black Wednesday" before Thanksgiving—and works a full shift loading bags onto planes. It's a good workout for him, but it's also a chance to connect with workers he knows are important contributors to the company's bottom-line results.

## Sometimes It's Tough Being Nice

The philosophy that employees come first and customers second is a pretty bold thing to say to your staff. The wrong type of person could go on a power trip and take advantage of such thinking. But to us, it's real simple: Our focus as a company has to be on our employees, because if our employees are not happy, our customers aren't going to get decent service.

Sure, we have employees who make mistakes. And when they do, we apologize profusely, attempt to correct the problem, and try to win the customer back. On the other hand, customers today tend to be much more aggressive than they were in the past. Our flight attendants in particular have noticed that, over the last two or three years, passengers have become much more demanding. They seem to be angry when they walk onto a plane. I think it's because people's lives are so stressful. Just getting to the airport can be a hassle.

If you're in a customer service business, you have to be thick-skinned in this type of environment. You have to realize that when someone yells at you or calls you a name or is disrespectful to you, it's not really you they're angry with. They're upset with the situation.

Of course, we never expect our employees to accept physical or verbal abuse. If a customer starts cussing up a storm or tries to attack an employee—we've actually had customers come over the counter at our people—that's when we say good-bye and good riddance. We won't tolerate such behavior, and we don't want their business if that's how they're going to behave.

To deal with more aggressive behavior, in fact, we've had to revise the way we perform our services. For one thing, our training now addresses the different types of confrontations employees might find themselves involved in. We've been offering conflict resolution classes for about two years, and stress management classes for about five years. Most of these classes are optional, but we encourage them strongly. We also now conduct mandatory "customer care" classes each year, the most recent of which focused on internal customer service and was called "Mind the Gap."

As we identify trends and themes throughout the year, we integrate learning opportunities to address the issues. We ask what skills or knowledge are lacking and what behaviors must change to determine the appropriate training or other intervention to take. Many employees say the information helps them not only on the job but also with personal communication. When employees have the appropriate skills, knowledge, and support, they are more confident in dealing with customers, even irate ones.

We spend hundreds of thousands of dollars each year on customer service training. One program I'm very excited about is our new supervisor training process, which addresses all the basic skills and tools necessary to be successful on the job. The program is called QUEST, and it took more than a year and a half to develop. It addresses specific relevant, job-related examples and provides opportunities for analysis and practice on how to handle problematic encounters.

I'm getting fantastic feedback on QUEST. A customer service manager told me, for example, that one of her new supervisors was returning from a QUEST class when she happened upon an agent who was verbally abusing a supervisor of eight years in front of several other employees in a break room. The veteran supervisor was intimidated and not handling the situation very well. The new supervisor stepped in, defused the situation, and made it possible for both employees to walk away with their principles intact. The new supervisor was especially excited because she had practiced something that had been taught to her in class—and it worked magnificently!

Learning how to discipline people can be one of the toughest challenges for our managers—especially new, first-time supervisors. We talk so much about being kind to one another that managers confronted with a disciplinary situation sometimes feel conflicted about being firm and being kind. It's similar to what parents feel when they struggle between wanting to spoil their children and needing to discipline them. In these cases, I remind managers that not disciplining employees pulls the whole work group down. Sometimes, I insist, you just have to practice tough love.

It's crucial, too—and, again, this might be perceived as a conflict—that you closely observe employees during probation and get rid of anybody about whom you have concerns. This is not to say that you shouldn't mentor and coach and try to teach employees the proper attitude. But during the probation period, which is usually about ninety days, a person's best foot should always be forward.

There are no formal training procedures or tricks used to determine if a person is a good fit for Southwest. The determination is made from observing each employee during his or her probation period, evaluating both on-job performance and interactions with co-workers and customers. If questions arise about someone's fit with Southwest, we almost always let him or her go. Every time you don't, you risk hurting the rest of the work team.

## MANAGERS WHERE THEY'RE NEEDED

The goal of customer service is to take care of a problem at the point of occurrence, not to pass it along to someone else to deal with later. Our policy is to have at least one manager in every city whose job it is to handle customer service issues as they happen. A great deal of this manager's time is spent conducting employee meetings and training sessions.

The station manager, the operations and ramp manager, and the customer service manager at each location work as a team, pinch-hitting for one another when necessary. We aim to have at least one manager on duty anytime a station is open, and all of them should be cross-trained to handle just about anything that comes up. We have developed these actions over the years as we realize that it's unfair to our people not to employ them, particularly during holiday times. Not only should we never stop empowering employees, but we should always have one person on hand who isn't afraid to make decisions that may cost the company money when it's the right thing to do.

## The Southwest Way

When Southwest started, we had a pretty simple and streamlined operating model: just three cities and a straightforward routine. Not much could go wrong, and with limited task training required of employees, they were freed up to concentrate on customer interactions.

We still strive to keep things simple, even though our system is much bigger now and stretches across the United States. Since we're not too dependent on computers, we probably have fewer things that can break down and disrupt service. I do fly on other airlines, and I know that when their computers break down, they practically come to a standstill. If our computers went down, I think we could still board airplanes without missing too many beats.

I guess you might say that we provide service in the old-fashioned, high-touch way—rather than relying on high technology. Nevertheless, we score very high in Department of Transportation (DOT) measures of the three areas of service: baggage handling, on-time performance, and customer complaints. We won the so-called Triple Crown for five straight years (1992–96), and no other carrier has ever won in all three categories even once since the DOT started tracking the air-travel consumer report in 1987. We have the best cumulative record for baggage handling over the past six years (through 1997) and have been ranked number one in customer satisfaction seven straight years.

## CUSTOMERS KNOW THE DRILL

One of the contributing factors to our superior on-time service record is that we have so many repeat flyers. Our customers understand our system fairly well, and as a result, they become some of our best spokespeople. For example, I spend a lot of time observing people in airport lounges. It really pleases me when I see someone who is a new flyer with us getting an explanation from one of our regulars as to what we're all about—and I see it all the time.

One of my favorite instances happened when we were opening Albuquerque. Herb Kelleher was standing in line to board the plane, talking to passengers as usual. This little old lady tapped him on the shoulder and said, "Young man, you better get on this airplane. This airline doesn't wait for anybody!" She knew the rules, and she wanted to make sure that her fellow passengers (even one who, unbeknownst to her, happened to be the CEO) all made the boarding call.

Our twenty-minute turnarounds are also largely made possible by our customers. Other carriers, who have turns averaging from forty-five minutes up to an hour or more, try to figure out how we do it. But I think that other than the obvious can-do attitude of our employees, the secret of the quick turns is that we have our customers well trained. The truth of the matter is that when people don't have an assigned seat, many get very nervous about it, so they get on the plane quickly to make sure they get a seat.

We capitalize on our ability to do quick turns by staying away from the busiest airports. We don't fly to airports such as New York's JFK, Washington National, and Boston's Logan that are famous—famous for horrible air and ground congestion problems. If we have to sit on the runway for forty minutes waiting for clearance to take off, we lose everything that we put into the twenty-minute turn.

## CYBER-TICKETING

Over 50 percent of our customers now use ticketless travel, many of them purchasing their seats by accessing our Website (www.southwest.com). The Web is fairly new to us, but it's working quite well and our customers seem to like it. The ticketless concept came about because we were never an active participant in the large carriers' customer reservations systems (CRS). We just felt their costs were prohibitive. They charge you for every segment they book, whether the person flies it or not.

We basically felt—particularly so in the early days—that because our service was so superior to that of our competitors, customers would insist on flying with us. We made it very easy. They basically just came out to the airport and got on the airplane. They didn't have to call and hold for twenty minutes to get a reservations agent.

When two of the three reservations systems that pretty much cover the United States announced that they were actually going to cut us out so that passengers who called them couldn't book us, we had to come up with an alternative quickly. Ticketless travel was our answer. It was entirely employee created and driven, and it has worked very well.

We are also in the process of developing a brand-new reservations system, the first in the industry in twenty-five years. I think this system will dramatically improve both our customer service package and our productivity, making it far easier and quicker to make a reservation on Southwest. And because it depends on internal computer technology, customers will not notice the transition to the new system—except in the speed with which their reservations are handled.

## CUSTOMERS ARE FAMILY, TOO

Each of our customers is obviously very important to us, but to find out exactly how much customers mattered, we conducted a study that appeared in the November 1995 edition of our company newsletter, *LUV Lines*. We found that a flight made during 1994 became profitable only after seventy-five passengers boarded, and that only five passengers per flight—or three million of the forty million passengers Southwest carried that year—accounted for the line's total annual profit of over $179.3 million. So losing just one passenger per flight because of bad service would reduce our profits by 20 percent.

One-on-one contact with customers, then, takes on added significance for us. Among the ways we seek to personalize our service is through our frequent flyer program known as "Rapid Rewards." The Southwest frequent flyer program is one of the easiest and simplest in the industry and allows us to track the number of trips people take. This, in turn, tells us who our best repeat customers are. Customers carry a plastic ID card that is swiped each time they check in for a flight, and they are sent quarterly statements that update them on their progress toward reaching various rewards.

It's very easy to get a free ticket. You don't even have to call and request it. After sixteen one-way trips in a consecutive twelve-month period, you automatically receive a free ticket in the mail, good for round-trip service between any two city pairs in our market. The program is very successful.

Another out-of-the-ordinary thing we do for our Rapid Reward members is to send them birthday cards. That may sound like the corniest thing, but you cannot imagine the response we get. Herb actually gets letters from people who say, "My mother didn't even send me a birthday card!"

## UNUSUAL CAMARADERIE

Because we offer such high-frequency service between most of our city pairs markets, we have customers who practically live with us. Many of our employees largely work the same shifts on a regular basis, so people who commute to work in a distant city five days a week come to know our flight attendants and ticket agents by name—and our people know them by name, too.

This practice is pretty unusual for the airline business, and it means I get calls quite regularly from both sides of the counter. A customer might call to say, "I haven't seen Sally at Gate 3 for the last couple of weeks. Is she all right?" Or a ticket agent will tell me, "Joe Jones has flown on us five days a week for seventeen years, and he's in the hospital with a heart attack," or he's retiring, moving, whatever. "Can we send him a gift?" So I reinforce a lot of one-to-one customer/employee relationships.

Our employees become like the newspaper guy on the street corner or the guy at the coffee cart whom you pass on your way to work every day. I can't imagine that many companies get letters from customers saying, "You have a new policy about carry-on bags and your employees don't like it. I want you to stop it because they're not happy." I get those kinds of letters all the time, and of course, whenever possible, we reexamine our policies to see if there is some way of accommodating customers, employees, and the people who make the regulations.

We were the David struggling against Goliath for so long that customers developed a proprietary feeling toward us, whether they were shareholders or not. They consider themselves—and rightfully so—responsible for our success. But along with that, the atmosphere that pervades Southwest has made them very comfortable about providing us with feedback, both good and bad.

People also just expect so much more from us. Some of the good PR that we've enjoyed does tend to cause problems from time to time. The more publicity you get, the higher people's expectations are for you. And every flight attendant on our system is not going to get on the PA and sing songs. That's one of the things that I talk to new hires about. I encourage them to feel comfortable with who they are so that they can strike a balance between their individuality and what the public expects.

## WHEN THINGS GO WRONG

Of the thousands of letters we receive each month, the complimentary mail far outweighs the negative by about five to one. This ratio is unusual, given the fact that people don't tend to sit down and write compliments to corporations. We do, of course, receive letters describing bad experiences. As often as possible, individual customer problems are met swiftly and succinctly. Each letter is answered personally by a company representative, and each issue is addressed carefully. If a flight was late, for example, the respondent checks the flight logs for the day and time referred to and determines the reason. If a flight attendant was rude, the employee's record is checked to see how many complaints have previously been logged against the attendant.

Once we find out the reason for the problem, this information is passed on to the customer. A letter might read something like this: "Your plane was late because bad weather in Kansas City kept it grounded for an extra hour before it could take off. As for the rude attendant, we have noticed that after five years of perfect conduct, that individual has received three complaints in one month's time. We will be meeting with her immediately to see what might be wrong."

All customer calls or letters are logged and tracked. I

have a customer relations department comprising about seventy people, and I also have a small group of thirteen to fifteen writers in my own office who handle specifics. For inquiries, requests, and everything else that comes to Herb or me, we try to get out a response in writing within four weeks.

When our mail began to increase dramatically as we added new cities, we started sending a postcard acknowledging receipt of a letter. If the letter requires any kind of investigation or report, we tell the correspondent not to be surprised if he doesn't hear from us for about four weeks because we want to do a thorough investigation before getting back with the facts. It's very rare that we lose touch. After discovering the facts of a case, we contact the customer again to explain how we resolved the issue.

I get monthly reports from the customer relations department so I can track trends in customer complaints. Another kind of tracking allows us to know if these dissatisfied customers have ever called before. We do a pretty good job of logging that. If a person has called three, four, or five times, it might just be a crank, or maybe it's valid, but it helps to be able to say, "I see that you also called last month."

## CUSTOMERS TRIGGER BETTER PRACTICES

Sometimes a customer suggestion or complaint leads to a very productive change. Here's a case in point. About five or six years ago we came up with a new policy that we called "One Stop Boarding." Previously, to get on the airplane, you showed up at the gate, handed over your ticket, and received a boarding card. We boarded in groups of thirty passengers, but you could never just go to the gate and get directly on the airplane. You had to stop at least once at the gate to get your boarding pass. On other airlines, if you had bought your ticket in advance, more than likely you would have your boarding pass already in hand when you arrived at the gate.

When our passengers had bags to check, they first had to stop either at the skycap or the ticket counter before going to the gate—where they had to stop again and stand in another line to get their boarding pass. With all these inconveniences in mind, we came up with One Stop Boarding. This service made it possible to check in at the ticket counter, where you could also get your boarding pass. Then you would not have to check in again at the gate.

We thought this was great—a real convenience for our customers. Well, they hated it. It took me weeks to figure out why: For years, our passengers had been conditioned to expect that arrival at the airport an hour in advance would put them in that first boarding group of thirty. They knew that if they went to their gate and waited for the ticket agent to open the flight, they were assured of getting the seat of their choice on the airplane.

When we started allowing people to get boarding passes at the ticket counter as well as at the gate, there were still customers sitting at the gate waiting to get boarding pass number one or two while forty other people who had already picked up passes at the ticket counter were off having a cup of coffee in the lounge. When the people who still waited realized they no longer had an advantage, they were just furious. They were so used to the old way of doing things that they made out like we were un-American for changing it. They were so vocal in their displeasure that we finally said "This isn't worth it" and abandoned the program.

Whether the same thing would happen today, I don't know. The more spread out we become, the more people we encounter who don't like our boarding process. They have to really get used to it. You have to remember that for the first several years of our existence, we were only an intrastate carrier. Our Texas customers knew our operation as well as we did. They knew everything about it, and they knew everything about how to make it work for them. All of our complaints about the one-stop boarding, by the way, were coming from Texas.

The no-meals policy, on the other hand, doesn't seem to generate complaints—even though people are more stressed out and more demanding. The only time we run into problems is when a customer just doesn't know about the policy before boarding. In the past, we held to the notion that you don't advertise a negative. So we didn't offer the no-meals information to people when they made reservations.

We've since changed our philosophy, however, and now advise customers of the policy when they call for a reservation. A little screen icon pops up to alert the reservations agent if a person is planning to take a fairly long trip on Southwest; the agent then knows to point out that we don't offer meal service and can encourage the customers to bring a sandwich on board.

## OUR PEOPLE ARE THE FUTURE

The biggest challenge that we have internally is to make the correct promotional decisions at the first-line supervisory level, and then to train properly and give our employees the tools to do their jobs.

As for customers, everyone has to spend more time advocating than they used to. And truthfully, our whole emphasis on customer service probably places us at the forefront. I get hundreds of letters each month that basically say, "I didn't think there was customer service left in this world and your agent proved me wrong. Your people make flying fun again."

## LIFE AFTER HERB

Although Herb has no intention of stepping down anytime soon, at some point, of course, both he and I will retire. I sure don't think the topic deserves the attention it seems to generate, but the world is obsessed with the idea of Herb retiring and Southwest being unable to function without him. I'm not taking anything away from Herb because he has been a wonderful leader. But the truth of the matter is, Herb cannot be in fifty-two locations on a regular basis. He cannot talk to the millions of passengers that we carry on a regular basis. It's the entire employee workforce that does those things now, and will continue to do them in the future.

In terms of our senior management leadership, we have a broad range of ages. We probably have the best team of officers now that we've ever had. Herb has done a heck of a good job hiring people who share our general outlook on life. What's more, there's not just one level of potential successors. There are probably two, depending on the time frame we're talking about.

Here's the bottom line: The spirit of Southwest is bigger than any individual, even if that individual is Herb Kelleher. What makes for long-term security, not just in the airline industry but in any industry, is good customer service provided by a loyal and committed workforce. In an industry where flight schedules and ticket fares determine whether planes fly full or half-full, it is excellence in customer service that sets Southwest Airlines apart from the competition.

■ ■ ■

## SOUTHWEST AIRLINES COMPANY

### COMPANY PROFILE

| | |
|---|---|
| Business Description | Airline |
| Website | www.iflyswa.com |
| Founded | 1967 |
| Annual Sales | $3.8 billion |
| Net Income | $317 million |
| Employees | 22,944 |
| Products | Safe, low-fare air travel |

*If you didn't know Southwest Airlines, could you imagine traveling on a carrier that doesn't serve meals on board, offers no reserved seating, operates with only half the number of employees per passenger that other airlines require, and is so picky about on-time departures that it cuts customers very little slack? Wouldn't you feel rushed? Wouldn't it feel like traveling in a cattle car?*

*Now suppose you were offered a chance to work for this airline. Imagine being asked to turn around planes twice as fast as the competition, with sometimes half the staff of the competition and with nothing much to offer the customer beyond a no-frills, low-fare ride? Wouldn't you do a double-take before signing on?*

*Put in that light, Southwest's accomplishments are even more marvelous—and the pivotal role of its people and customer service all the more essential. Customer service is the balancing act that juggles the company's superrational, lean business processes with the reality of emotional customers, unpredictable weather, and other wild cards. Customer service is the in-between that makes both the operating model and the customer hum.*

*With service excellence being so vital, it's not surprising that Southwest places such emphasis on shaping its distinct customer culture. Take another look at its hiring and training practices, then ask yourself these questions: Would you contemplate hiring newcomers to your industry who are often inexperienced but have the aptitude and imagination to enrich your unique orientation to customer service? Or would you rather hire veterans who have been groomed in your competitors' processes and culture?*

*Do you give your people as much latitude to get the job done right as Southwest does? Or does your obsession with running smooth operations compel you to run every activity by the book—proceduralizing, regimenting, and controlling every move?*

*Are you routinely rotating people through jobs? Do your managers go on multiple field visits per year, working in jobs they normally don't get exposed to? Or is your policy one of keeping everyone to his or her own business?*

*Nurturing a culture goes beyond hiring and training, of course. It requires constant communication to inform, remind, and reinforce people about "the way we do things here." Here are some tips about how to get your message across the Southwest way:*

- Use evocative titles. Do you have an executive vice president of customers? How about a People Department? A Culture Committee? A *Spirit* magazine? A stock market ticker name such as "LUV"?
- Celebrate camaraderie and teamwork. Play up your staff experiences. Promulgate stories that capture the spirit. Put emotion and feeling in the business, and the chances are you will get passionate employees.
- Don't forget to get your CEO or president to work a full shift loading bags on the busiest travel day of the year.

*And to top off all that, constantly remind yourself how important each customer is to your business performance:*

- Collect, scrutinize, and act on any customer input and feedback you can get hold of.
- Figure out how much difference one customer can make. At Southwest, remember, the break-even point is seventy-five customers per plane. So with an average load of eighty customers, it's only those last five that earn the company its profits. Have you done a similar calculation for your organization? If not, I strongly advise you to do so. You're likely to see some scary numbers that will redouble your effort to become more customer-oriented.

# 2

## Charles Schwab & Company, Inc.

*Invest in Trust*

F ounded in 1974, just a year before a ruling by the Securities and Exchange Commission (SEC) deregulated commissions in the securities business, Charles Schwab & Company, Inc., currently controls half the discount brokerage business in the United States. Schwab's success results from the value proposition instilled by Charles Schwab, founder and namesake, that customers would rather have low-cost, no-frills service than the speculative advice of a fast-talking broker. The logic works. Opening more than a hundred thousand new accounts each month, Schwab has an annual attrition level of just 6 percent—and most of the customers who leave the company go to fully commissioned brokerage firms rather than to other discounters.

Schwab has stayed on top by remaining innovative and customer-focused as competition in discount brokering has heated up during the 1990s. Its TeleBroker service allows *clients to trade stocks via Touch-Tone telephone; its VoiceBroker system enables those same customers to call in for stock quotations and to trade mutual funds through voice recognition. Both are widely popular: TeleBroker takes in six million monthly calls (many in Mandarin Chinese, Cantonese Chinese, and Spanish), and VoiceBroker accounts for another one million calls per month. Schwab also utilizes the power of the Internet to offer its clients several ways to manage their money on-line, with trading available through Schwab's Website (www.schwab.com) for $29.95 per trade.*

*Diversification is another secret to Schwab's success. In 1992, the company entered into an entirely new market area—no-transaction-fee/no-load mutual funds—through the establishment of its highly successful OneSource program. OneSource enables users to buy into any of 1,400 no-load funds through an existing Schwab account, without being charged the company's typical minimum transaction fee of $39. Before, it could take six days for investors to get a prospectus from a fund distributor and another three days after putting up their money before the purchase went through. OneSource now cuts the wait time down to a single phone call or Internet connection. And in addition to servicing current Schwab investors, OneSource enables the company to tap an entirely new customer base: fee-only financial advisors who manage client portfolios of stocks or no-load mutual funds themselves but receive trade processing, custody, technical, and administrative support from Schwab.*

*The result of these measures has been skyrocketing*

*growth. After taking twenty years to record $100 billion in total client assets, Schwab needed just two more years to reach $200 billion—then jumped all the way up to the $300 billion mark less than twelve months later. Schwab has changed with the times, to be sure, but it has never strayed from its fundamental value proposition: Give customers the opportunity to be their own financial planners and, at the same time, let them know a broker is always there if needed.*

## DAVID S. POTTRUCK

Co-CEO and President, The Charles Schwab Corporation

## REDEFINING AN INDUSTRY

### *Customer Service as a Value Proposition*

The story goes that Charles Schwab ("Chuck") decided early on that putting a face on the company—his face—would be a good idea. The photograph we used in our first ad featuring Chuck's picture was actually a photo taken of him by the *San Francisco Chronicle* for an article they ran. We bought the photograph and the rights to use it for $1.50, and it wound up appearing in all our early ads. When the response rate to the ads featuring Chuck's photo doubled, we realized there was something terrific about the way this guy looked. He just had this wonderful, all-American, trustworthy appearance. And putting a face on the company helped our customer connect with us and give our service a more personable feeling.

I think Schwab's journey in the area of customer service

has been an interesting evolution over more than twenty years. When the company was established, the notion was really that there was a segment of customers who didn't need the advice of a fully commissioned broker and didn't like the sales pressure such a broker often gave them.

That reasoning pushed us to redefine what brokerage advice is all about. Fully commissioned brokers have developed the concept of "advice" to mean they can predict the exact direction the market will take over the next 30, 60, 90, or 180 days. Then they offer investors tips on which "hot stocks" will generate skyrocket returns. That's not what we do. We believe that people really want an advisor who can demystify investing. They want a person to help them figure out what to do next—and how to do it—in a way that makes the process simpler and empowers the customer to take control. They don't want to rely too heavily on us or feel they can't make a move without our telling them what to do.

Accordingly, we have conversations with our customers, trying our best to stay in touch with them through various channels of communication. We don't just focus on their problems and tune out the rest of their calls.

We remind ourselves every day that the press tends to see what discount brokers do as a commodity. You just place a trade, and there's a price you pay for it. The press can't figure out how we can expect to grow unless we charge the lowest price. They miss the intangible of service in this business. Customers don't, however. They feel it. They experience it.

Our company was founded on the principle that we would have dramatically reduced prices and relatively bare-bones service. In fact, our original slogan was "Charles Schwab, the transaction specialist." We thought of ourselves as just that. You called us to make a transaction, and we put it through seamlessly, accurately, and consistently. And that was that.

By 1980, we were still an incredibly small company with revenues of less than $50 million. Then we decided to make things even easier for our customers by installing an automated system to support our brokers and getting away from writing paper tickets. At the time, every brokerage firm in the industry, including Merrill Lynch, was writing paper tickets. But we envisioned on-line order entry, on-line customer balances, and on-line information as a way to provide better customer service. Now that vision has come true. Today if customers are traveling, for instance, they can call into any Schwab branch for information and be assured that whoever answers the call has the same access to their accounts as the Schwab broker they deal with at home.

We can't say that we fully anticipated the role computers and eventually the Internet were going to play in today's business environment. I would say we were more like Columbus setting sail to the Orient, bumping into America, and then being remembered as this great discoverer. We set out to keep costs down, and what we have discovered over a twenty-year period is that we've built a reputation as a technology-based service and retailing firm that happens to be in the brokerage business.

Of course, this technology doesn't mean a thing if you don't have the people up front supporting it and establishing contact with customers. Our brokers have the same licenses as traditional Wall Street retail brokers and, in many cases, more experience. Just as important, the employees who make first contact with potential customers understand the basic culture of our firm.

I believe that in almost any company, customer service has to start in the hearts of the people who serve those clients. You have to build an organization around people who like helping customers. You can train people how to do it, but I frankly believe that people are born with this interest—or maybe early experiences in their lives lead them there. People either like being in service to other people, or they don't.

## STRIVING TO BE USEFUL AND ETHICAL

Schwab values fairness, empathy, and responsiveness. We constantly strive to innovate and improve everything we do, building on the power of teamwork and trying always to be worthy of our customers' trust. Five or six years ago, when we began developing this vision, my personal goal was to get every employee in the company to take it to heart—not just repeat it as Corporatespeak, but repeat it as something he or she believed in. Schwab builds its value proposition around its principle of customer service. I think that's why we've attracted so many financial assets from our customers. Our customer assets at Schwab have grown by roughly 40 percent annually over the past ten plus years, and in 1997 we blasted right up to $354 billion in total assets. Even with an unkind market during the second half of the year, 1997 marked the first time we exceeded $100 billion in asset growth during a single calendar year. Needless to say, that's incredibly huge momentum. We believe that our high level of service inspires the kind of trust our customers show in us, and that this trust results in more growth by the company.

Fair pricing is a large part of the value we offer. We've lowered our pricing dramatically in recent years. Once upon a time, if you bought a mutual fund here at Schwab, you paid us a transaction fee equal to about one-half of 1 percent of the size of your transaction. On an average transaction of roughly $10,000, that computed to about a $50 charge. When we launched OneSource, we eliminated those charges. We got the funds to pay us. And although the funds pay us less than the customer used to pay, this arrangement allowed us to provide a free service. We also took our IRA fee a few years ago from $29 to zero for all IRAs above $10,000. And at the same time we've dropped our rates, our customer service levels have actually increased.

There's no question that preservation of core values is an enormously challenging task. We never wrote any of this down until 1991, when I mentioned to Chuck that we needed to codify the vision and values of our company.

"Why do we need to do that?" he asked. "Everybody I talk to already knows them."

"But, Chuck," I said, "we have three thousand employees. You can't talk to all of them. The ones you do talk to understand the vision and values because they hang around you and hear them. But we have a lot of other employees who have never met you. And we're hiring more and more people from the industry, who bring with them their cultures and values from other companies. It's important that we begin this process of acculturation."

So in 1991, for the first time, we wrote down our vision and values. Our stated vision, first articulated by Chuck, was "to be the most useful and ethical brokerage firm in America." Because of the way our services are changing and because we've become more of a global company, our vision statement has since evolved. We now seek "to be the most useful and ethical financial services firm in the world." The values of the firm—to be a fair, empathetic, responsive, trustworthy group striving to innovate through the power of teamwork—have stayed the same. What has changed are our strategic priorities, the guiding efforts that help us achieve the mission. Every four or five years, we find ourselves updating our set of priorities.

Today we have 12,500 employees, but we deal with them in a more efficient manner than we did back in 1991, when we had 3,000. That's because we now train our staff to be empathetic and to earn customers' trust. Our best recruits, those who stay and love it here, are individuals who like the notion of helping and being in service to customers. We believe our mission is noble: to be the custodians of our customers' financial dreams. Our customers rely on us to help them with the things that are most important to them—retirement, a home, a college education for their children. Those are the three most frequently reported reasons for people opening accounts and investing for the future, and we help our customers achieve those goals. If we do a great job of that, they reward us with more business, refer other people to us, and enable us to grow and expand.

When we survey current and past customers, we know exactly what they want—and why they leave. Interestingly, remarkably few customers leave to go to deeper discounters. We lose more customers to firms that promise to give them surefire advice. Perhaps these customers have come across more money or think they've mismanaged the money they have, and they want someone to give them guarantees. Well, we don't do that.

We're not interested in high-pressure salesmen, and we're not interested in customer service people who don't know how to use customer service as an opportunity and a permission to ask for more business. Frankly, you can't provide great customer service, be there for customers, answer their questions, and grab the phone in thirty to forty seconds with a well-trained person on the line and still charge $15 or less for a trade.

We have to figure out how to make investing easier for our customers and get better at giving these customers help and advice so that we can increase the success of their investments. If we're to play the role of custodians of our customers' financial dreams, we don't want that to be a passive role. We want to be active, to add our own expertise while we follow their lead. We want customers to trust us and feel that we've made a difference in their lives.

## WHERE IT BEGINS

People interested in seeking jobs with our company can use our Website (www.schwab.com) to get more information and guidance. As the headline over the recruiting portion of the site clearly states, "We're looking for employees who put customers first." In all our interviews, we listen for the things people say that suggest noble service on behalf of customers is what they do best. One thing that interests us is a person's involvement in charitable giving and community service. We look for that in employees—the notion of giving back, of making a difference. Schwab is tremendously involved in supporting this culture at all levels of the company.

We've put a lot of effort into revamping our orientation program for new employees. From the minute you join Schwab, there is a strong acculturation process. We used to concentrate on teaching new hires about the organizational structure of the firm—how to fill out forms to order stationery, how to get phone numbers of other employees, that kind of stuff. Today, we do a lot less basic instruction. After all, most organizational information is on our Intranet system, where employees can look it up when they need it. Instead, we spend most of our time helping employees understand what the company stands for, what we're trying to accomplish, and how we expect them to treat one another—and treat our customers—so that we all speak with one voice.

For example, we don't put an inexperienced broker right out of training on the phone with customers, handling trades and things of that nature. Our somewhat hierarchical system works people through the business, starting them in places where they have less customer impact, then eventually letting them make their way to the phones.

A big part of our phone training is teaching our brokers to look for the different signals a customer gives that provide insight into how he or she can best be served. Each time a customer contacts us, for instance, we want our brokers to get some idea of which service is most appropriate to fit his or her immediate needs. What kind of investor is this customer? Is she very active? Is she relatively inactive? Is she a mutual fund customer? Is she a wealthy customer who needs many services? Or is she a beginning investor, who might have $5,000 to $10,000 to spend and whose investment choices and problems are much simpler? Our brokers are trained to distinguish these differences early and act accordingly.

To aid in this process, brokers at all our branches are trained to apply a risk analysis and asset allocation process to each customer who asks for help in forming an investment strategy. It takes only a few minutes but serves as a great way to determine the most appropriate direction for each customer to go in. Say you're brand new to investing and don't possess much knowledge, but you want to learn.

Our broker might suggest that the most reasonable thing to do would be to get your feet wet with mutual funds because of the obvious advantages—the investment doesn't take much capital, someone else is picking the securities, and there are a lot of funds to choose from. The broker would probably suggest an index fund as the core of the portfolio because it offers a certain amount of predictability and exposes you to equity markets in a broadly diversified way.

As we earn their trust over time, customers begin to share with us the more intimate issues of their financial lives. The task for brokers at this point is to problem-solve unobtrusively, again attempting to figure out what kind of Schwab services would be most appropriate for each customer. This is a key part of a new broker's training. Although we never openly talk about or advertise ourselves as "custodians of our customers' financial dreams," we want our people to think of themselves in those terms. It's what we strive to instill in each new employee.

Even those individuals who have been in the brokerage business at the big, full-commission brokerage firms for several years still have a lot to learn about how Schwab does things. Our training process and the consistency of our service delivery has gotten better and better in the face of massive hiring over the past couple of years. Approximately half of our employees are licensed brokers working directly with customers on a regular basis. There are a lot of other people at headquarters who wish to pursue their brokerage license even though they don't work as Schwab brokers, and we encourage it. In fact, the company pays for their training and annual licenses and provides the educational materials they need. We know that although they may work in advertising, marketing, or operations, these employees will better serve customers if they have a greater understanding of our core business. And serving the customer as well as possible is the bottom line, no matter what department you're in.

## BENCHMARKING: HELPING FORM CORE VALUES

We're not bound by traditional industry stereotypes, and we recognize that learning often comes from studying non-traditional models of business. We pay close attention to the Wal-Marts, Home Depots, Intels, and Microsofts. They understand notions of customer service, innovation, and the use of technology in a way that, until recently, was relatively transparent to the customer. Today, our customers are in touch with technology; in the past, this aspect of the business was in the shadows. All the customers knew was that they received incredibly reliable, high-quality, consistent service at a remarkably low price. Technology has always been in the picture, of course, but never more so than today.

When you look at Home Depot or Wal-Mart, for example, you see companies with employees who really feel strongly about the organization, what it stands for, and what it's trying to do. I own stock in those companies myself, and I go through their annual reports to learn what I can. I've also spent a brief amount of time with Arthur Blank, the president and CEO of Home Depot, and I talked to him about some of these issues.

Home Depot is a firm that tries to offer incredibly low prices while at the same time training employees well enough to provide the highest level of customer service. As a customer, you get low prices without having to sacrifice service. Home Depot isn't just lumber and nails. The employees of the company take to heart the notion that their mission is to help you with your home.

Another interesting idea I got from Home Depot is the way it services different types of customers. My dad, who's a contractor, once pointed out to me that if you go to Home Depot at 7:00 A.M., the parking lot is full of contractors. They've all gone off to their job sites by 10:00 A.M., and then it's home owners who are in the store, looking to do their own improvements. So while Home Depot serves both the professional and the private citizen, the company handles each with different types of customer service.

At times this can lead to conflicts. A contractor, for instance, might be inclined to say to a Home Depot employee, "Yeah, you sell me lumber, but, you know, you're also helping people do this for themselves. You're putting me out of business." Home Depot walks the fine line of serving both sides of that market, just as we do in serving professional money managers who supervise individual portfolios as well as the individual investors themselves.

## ELIMINATING COMMISSIONS AS AN
## EMPLOYEE MOTIVATOR

I think our incentive systems are particularly interesting. As most people are aware, our competition pays commissions to their salespeople. Those commissions are fundamentally driven not by whether customers make money, not by whether they remain loyal, but simply by how often they trade. It's all about how much of their money brokers can move around.

Here at Schwab, we don't pay people commissions at all. None of our brokers or customer-service people earns money for getting customers to trade more or less. In fact, the frequency with which our customers trade is not part of the employee reward system—because it's not related to whether the employee is more successful. We relate our rewards to the assets our customers bring into our company. So the more our customers bring money to Schwab and the less they take money out of Schwab—that's the fundamental driver of our quarterly incentive system. The huge focus here is on the customer's trust in us. We separate the issue of market depreciation or decline from net new money coming into the company.

We're not interested in our brokers selling the "product of the day." We're after overall asset growth. This can mean bringing in more business from already existing customers. Let's say a customer had a bunch of mutual funds scattered all over the place. The broker could let the customer know that we offer a marketplace and that clients can transfer all of their mutual funds here so that they are valued on one monthly statement and one 1099 form come tax season. That's considered new business. If and when the customer decides to trade out some nonperforming mutual funds and invest in something new, we count on that money remaining here at Schwab.

We also determine quarterly employee rewards mostly by the way customers judge the service they have received. Ten percent of our customers—chosen at random—receive telephone surveys that we code and track back to the team that served those customers to evaluate how well they were treated. We study these ratings when they come back in, then combine them with the amount of money each broker team has brought into Schwab. Based on the combination of those two factors, we then reward our brokers and service people.

Let's say the goal for a Schwab branch is $125 million a year in new assets. You achieve your goal and come in right on target—100 percent goal, $125 million. Then we look at your customer service score. If your service scores are exceptional, you get an even higher bonus. But if your service scores are below a certain level, your bonus is wiped out. You get zero. If you don't provide strong service, the fact that you brought in a lot of money doesn't matter. That's an extreme example, of course, and it doesn't happen very often. But it gets the message across that customer service is the sine qua non of our business. The idea is to inextricably intertwine customer service and asset generation. If people do a great job on customer service and generating trust, but they fail to use this to gain permission to ask for more business, then they are doing only half their job.

We've tweaked our incentive system for years, but its fundamental focus has been remarkably consistent and still works well. Nobody says, "I make money when my customers lose money," or "I have to be manipulative moving someone's money around so that I can make my mortgage payment this month." Again, unlike our competitors, everyone here is on a salary. There's none of this huge pressure that you will be starting at zero each month and have to earn commission. You always have your salary, and the bonuses can be quite substantial—anywhere from 10 percent to 50 percent of base pay. So there's an ample amount of leverage.

You don't see a lot of emphasis on profitability in our mission, in our vision statement, in our strategic priority statement—all the things that help our frontline employees understand what it is we're trying to do. In a sense, profitability is a measure of whether our executive management has architectured our firm appropriately and invested in the right initiatives. Certainly, we all recognize how important profitability is. But we believe that for employees who directly service customers, profitability should be an outcome rather than a motive. It should come at the end of a job rather than up front, driving our thoughts every day.

## PUTTING EMPLOYEE IDEAS TO WORK

We have a great process for soliciting employee ideas on how to fix problems and serve customers better. We put out a field publication subtitled "News You Can Use." It's a way for management to both share ideas we have and get ideas from people on our front lines. I would guess that about 50 percent of the publication each month is contributed by people out in the field. We always have a feature called "The One That Got Away," in which someone contributes a story about an opportunity when, frankly, we didn't do what we should have done and lost either a new or an existing customer.

A recent article, for example, discussed the loss of a $5 million customer to rival Merrill Lynch because the Schwab representatives who dealt with the customer assumed the customer knew more about trading than he really did. By the time we learned the customer lacked a basic understanding of how orders are placed and executed, a friend had already convinced him to shift to Merrill Lynch. Although we called to let him know we could give him all the help he needed, his mind was made up. Cases like this one teach us to be careful about the assumptions we make regarding customers.

## DESIGNING A STRUCTURE FOR SERVICE

Through marketing and referrals, Charles Schwab currently opens up about a hundred thousand new accounts a month on an unsolicited basis. None of these accounts is gained from cold calls; every one is a customer who has come to us. These clients have existing accounts and want. to open another, or they represent a new household that would like to establish a relationship with us.

Each account is assigned to a branch office—the location of which appears on the customer's monthly statement. We have more than 270 branch offices throughout the United States, each with the primary mission of further enhancing customer relationships. There are Schwab offices in every major city, set up to handle walk-in traffic and spend time building relationships and helping established customers. Most basic transactions are also handled through a variety of other channels, including our four service centers, operation centers, the Internet, our Touch-Tone TeleBroker system, and our VoiceBroker voice-recognition system.

This wasn't always the case. Turn back the clock ten years, and we had no service centers. We had no VoiceBroker, no TeleBroker, and no on-line network. The hundred or so branches we did have were in the customer service business out of necessity; all phone calls, transactions, customer service issues, and paper-processing needs were handled by them. There was nobody else to do the work.

Today, the branch offices may take 3 or 4 percent of our trading and customer service phone calls, but that's really the exception. As part of our transition from "the transaction specialist" to an organization promoting "investing the way it should be," branch brokers spend the majority of their time calling on new accounts to welcome them to the company. The brokers educate new clients on a variety of topics—from how to use our Touch-Tone and on-line systems to how to get detailed information about investing. Through a series of phone calls and get-togethers, they hopefully establish a strong rapport. Because Schwab employs only about five people at each branch, customers are likely to speak with the same two or three brokers each time they call or come in. This familiarity helps build trust.

Brokers at the service centers (located in Phoenix, Denver, Indianapolis, and Orlando) handle many routine orders by phone. A lot of people just want to buy or sell a few hundred shares of stock. Some are expecting a dividend in their account that didn't post; others have questions about "funny transactions" regarding a stock they recently sold. In such cases, the broker might simply explain that the transaction in question occurred because the dividend hit after the customer sold the stock, and Schwab had to take it out and send it to the new owner. Most of these inquiries can be solved with no trouble.

Then there are the more complicated calls that necessitate face-to-face meetings. A person might call and say, "I just got a rollover from my employee retirement plan. I came into $350,000, and I have no idea how to invest this much money. I would like to buy mutual funds and have heard about things like asset allocation. Can you explain this to me?" On a call like this, our employee would suggest the customer come into the branch nearest his or her home and work directly with one of our brokers. Each phone broker has a list of numbers and addresses for all our branches to help the customer find the most convenient location.

Think of it as total integration. No matter which channel you choose for doing business with us—automated phone, direct phone contact, a branch visit, or on a PC with our Internet site—everything is linked so that you get access to the same investments and the same kind of information you need to establish an account. A customer can choose to use any channel at any time, and he'll get account information and help.

## SYSTEMS GEARED TO WIN

Once we get all the pertinent information about a customer into our computer database, we really begin to know this person. We know the different accounts they have and something about what they're trying to accomplish. From this point on, when a person calls and speaks to one of our brokers, the broker can directly bring up onto the computer screen whatever information he or she needs about that customer. And because the data is universally accessible across the system, any one of our brokers can handle any customer call and still deliver the same level of personal service.

We discovered long ago that procedure manuals and reference books don't work well. They can't be kept up-to-date. Now we keep most procedure and reference information on-line, where our brokers can access it and we can update it regularly.

We have a system that we call IWIN, which stands for "I Want Information Now." If a customer calls in with specific procedural or reference questions, the agent handling the call asks what piece of Schwab material the caller is looking at, then checks the hundreds of pieces of literature in our IWIN network for an immediate answer.

Before IWIN, there was no quick way to get assistance when brokers were asked questions about material they were not familiar with. This often resulted in unproductive conversations. Agents can now look up a piece on-line, see what the caller is referring to, and explain it succinctly. If our employees have questions of their own, they can bring up a reference page that tells them everything they need to know about the service, how it works, how it's priced, who needs it, and other similar services. This has become an incredibly powerful system, and customers develop a sense of confidence and assurance when the Schwab broker can answer their questions knowledgeably.

## COMPLAINTS "R" US

Although we have what we call a "customer complaint" department, we like to think of it as the "customer retention" department. We want our people there to think that they are not just handling complaints, they are helping retain customers.

We actually measure the complaint department based on how much business customers do in the six months after they complain and we address their complaint versus the six months before they complained. We want our staff to realize that it's really not about whether we give an agitated customer a $50 credit but whether we keep the account and the person continues doing business with us. If we simply get the customer off our backs and he or she leaves, we haven't accomplished very much.

Since we started measuring this, we have found a remarkable improvement in our results as measured by customer behavior. More than half the customers we talk to actually do more business with us after we have serviced their complaint. So at the end of the day, we're doing pretty well, obviously, and that's one of the reasons our business is growing.

## A Group Effort

Our Service Enhancement Team—we sometimes call them "barrier bashers"—is a collection of people whose primary goal is to improve the quality of service to customers. After the market crashed in 1988, we had a huge decline in volume. Founding the Service Enhancement Team offered us a way to reclaim some of those losses. We realized then that we had a series of procedures in the company that can be called "scar tissue." In other words, something goes wrong and we write a procedure so that it never happens again. Over time, all this scar tissue from failures builds up until, suddenly, nobody feels able to serve a customer because so many rules and regulations make it almost impossible to give good service.

Most companies develop scar tissue similar to ours. Failures mount over time, and there is an imperfect healing. The cost of following a new procedure put in place to prevent some snafu from happening again is often higher than the original losses when you look at the inconvenience suffered by customers as a result. But you can't measure that beforehand.

The Service Enhancement Team often tries to solve problems that involve internal policies or procedures that get in the way of strong customer service because they were written by someone in headquarters whose purpose it was to protect the company or make sure that something wasn't done wrong. That customers might be inconvenienced was probably not thoroughly understood beforehand, and as a result the policy or procedure is largely unresponsive to the realities experienced in the field.

One concern our team addressed was the length of time required to resolve customer complaints. The process of determining responsibility for problems was taking too long; departments often argued about precisely where the mistakes were made and out of which group's budget the money to fix the mistakes needed to come. To solve this issue, the team created a streamlined process dubbed "Rapid Resolution" and established a customer service quality group to determine which department was responsible for each error—and its correction.

Customers themselves often bring these problems to our attention. One benchmarking effort with our customers revealed that although they did not expect Schwab to perform flawlessly, customers did want mistakes to be taken seriously and handled expeditiously. This effort also disclosed that customers wanted to work with one contact person during all their interactions with Schwab.

At the time customers were telling us this, our service-delivery organizations were focused more on enabling customer transactions and providing investment guidance and support than on problem resolution—especially when the problem involved time-consuming research. After we learned how customers felt, we assigned special teams in each regional service center to work closely with frontline representatives to investigate dilemmas and reassure customers. Staffers now take ownership of problems and at the same time keep the appropriate line departments informed of progress.

The Service Enhancement Team is run by a vice president who actually sits here in headquarters, but it is made up of people who have come from the field. So they have great empathy for what the field jobs are all about. You spend a couple years in service enhancement, and it's a great experience. It's very satisfying to figure out how to unravel a procedure so that it's more customer-oriented but still protects the company and captures the essence of the company's needs.

In 1996, the Service Enhancement Team identified, with the help of a customer survey, fifty troubling policies that most got in the way of our delivering stellar customer service. Team members had to figure out how to unravel these policies and either eliminate them or replace them with something less onerous. The list covered a variety of issues—things we needed to do better, procedures that didn't work, policies that got in the way, products we should have had but didn't—and we addressed each individually.

While this team addresses trends or issues that develop

into problems over time, individual customer complaints are handled as they come in by another department—the chairman's division. This group investigates incidents of customer dissatisfaction, then follows up each one with a phone call and letter to the customer. In situations in which a product is involved, the appropriate product team is alerted to look into modifications.

## Bringing the Customer into the Mix

The difference in the quality of service you receive from Schwab compared with the service you receive at other brokerage houses starts when you open an account. We believe there is no other company in the business that is as approachable without intimidation, or as accessible, inviting, and understanding of what is important to you. No matter what the size of your portfolio, we try to accommodate your needs.

Schwab is and has always been a conduit for information from unbiased third-party sources to our clients. That means we're not going to recommend any particular stocks, nor are we going to push any "get rich quick" schemes. What we are going to do is provide you with access to research sources that will enable you to make your own decisions. And no other discount broker offers you the level of personal interaction and guidance that is available from Schwab brokers—either in face-to-face meetings or by phone.

"Can you explain this limit order to me?" a customer might ask a broker. "What happens if the limit order doesn't go off? Do I still pay the commission? Is there anything I give up? When is the best time to use a limit order? What are the different strategies for limit orders versus market orders?" No matter what the situation, we would take the time to explain how it works.

It's the same if you're setting up an IRA account, doing an IRA rollover, setting up accounts for your children, or learning how to get distributions out of your account so that you can get a check each month after you retire. Or maybe you're thinking about investing in mutual funds. What could be easier than mutual funds? Well, today there are eight thousand mutual funds. There are more mutual funds than stocks on the New York Stock Exchange. So investing in mutual funds is not always easy. What we try to do is help simplify the process. And you're never going to get that service at another discount brokerage firm. It just doesn't exist.

## A HIGHER LEVEL OF HELP: SCHWAB 500

The size of your portfolio and the amount of business you do with us qualifies you for different levels of service. Customers who maintain a certain equity level and trade a minimum of four times per month qualify as Schwab 500 clients. Many of these traders are independent businesspeople who have decided to manage their own finances, and some are actually professional traders. These Schwab 500 clients get a tremendous amount of extra service, including the use of special service teams within Schwab that they can call on any time they want. Because many of our most active customers do more sophisticated trading, the service teams are essential in helping make sense of every aspect of a customer's portfolio.

If you are a Schwab 500 customer and want us to send or fax a lot of information on a company, we'll do it. If you want us to follow certain stocks more closely, we'll do so and call you when there's important news or a big movement you should know about. Using technology right on their desktops, members of the service team will walk you through trades, help you understand how to place your trade, look up the research, and tell you whether opinions on Wall Street have changed regarding your stock.

Some Schwab 500 client requests are stored in computers, which automatically alert service teams when predetermined guidelines are met. Brokers then pass the desired news on to interested clients. If seventy-five Schwab 500 clients request information about a particular IBM acquisition, for instance, a group fax will go out to those investors as soon as the deal is completed. Just think of it as institutional-quality service for the individual investor.

## No Gimmicks

Interestingly, we have no marketing program, procedures, sales programs, contests, or anything else in the company intended to push people toward making more trades. The customer is at his or her own discretion. We've realized that the better the investment information we give our customers, the more likely they are to be more successful and make more trades that generate additional revenue for us.

Accordingly, we've built the company around the idea that our goal is not to generate the maximum amount of revenue per dollar of assets that customers leave here. Because, in fact, all those revenues come out of the customer's pocket. We want to be respectful of that. The notion is that by generating a relatively small amount of revenue from each customer's portfolio, we can still make an adequate profit and the customer will receive great returns on his or her portfolio. Then, the hope is, the customer will reward us with more business (and maybe even referrals from friends!).

## SCHWAB ON-LINE (WWW.SCHWAB.COM)

We are the largest on-line broker, with 1.2 million active on-line accounts as of March 1998, and we're growing all the time. During the fourth quarter of 1997, on-line trades represented 41 percent of Schwab's total trades—up from 28 percent over the same period in 1996. Our number of on-line clients has tripled in two years, and we now get ten million hits a day on our Website. Total client assets of on-line customers at the end of 1997 was $80.3 billion, and more than $100 billion by March 1998. The industry is just exploding.

The great thing about the Internet is that you can find just about anything you want; the major problem is sorting it out to find what's best for you. People are inundated with information. Our goal is to get more into the business of helping people wade through all this information so that investing becomes easier for them. With this in mind, we're constantly increasing the number of services—most of them free—available on our Website.

Everybody from novice investors to our most advanced traders can get something out of the site. Some people use it for information only. Other people are mutual fund investors, so for them we put up mutual fund performance data, along with information on how to analyze and compare funds. Still other people use it for planning and guidance, so we've made available an asset allocation tool. From our Web-based customer center, Schwab clients can access account information, make trades, examine their transaction history, and get free stock quotes, news, and research.

Executing a trade on our site requires only two steps—accessing an account and placing the order. Even if you wish to take a quick glance at the company report, the views of some analysts, and the stock's historical price versus its moving average, the entire process takes a few minutes. And you can trade twenty-four hours a day, seven days a week. Just as we have worked to make our general pricing more fair, we've lowered the costs of conducting trades on-line. Using Schwab's Online Advantage Service, anybody with $2,500 in equity can open an on-line account and conduct trades for $29.95 each, up to one thousand shares. (Trades of more than one thousand shares cost three cents per extra share.)

A major concern for our clients is saving for their kids' college education. Using another free service on the Website, they can punch in the age of their children, the state in which they reside, and whether their children will likely attend a public or private institution. This data will immediately cue up an estimate of how much four years of college will cost when each of their children turns eighteen. Building on this information, the service goes on to offer advice on how to start an effective college savings plan, gives a variety of investment options, and provides the chance to open an account. Similar services are also available on the Web for retirement and general accounts.

The Website is a great learning tool as well. Even if you're someone who has heard about market orders and limit orders, you still might not know exactly what they are or how they work. It's there on the Website. Let's say you're thinking about what you want to do and you know a limit order is a choice. Push a button marked "Help," and the help screen explains to you what a limit order is. Then, if you still don't know if it's the right thing to do, you can pick up a phone and call a broker.

## LISTENING IN

Soliciting feedback is one of the most important things we do at the company, and it encompasses three steps: surveying customers, tracking the responses back to the Schwab agents who helped them, and meeting with those agents to reinforce strengths and work on problem areas. In 1985, we initiated the process of getting information directly from our customers via this three-step method. In the past, we just mailed a written survey to about 10 percent of customers for whom we had handled a transaction. Now, as the first step in the process, we survey about 10 percent of our customer base via telephone calls. Telephoning allows us to probe for greater detail in order to better understand what customers like and what they don't like. And we now do these surveys at random rather than poll only those who make a trade or open an account. We want to assess customers' satisfaction with their overall relationship with Schwab—not just the mechanics of doing trades.

Second, we take the results from these surveys and analyze them to use as a training tool. The survey call gives customers the opportunity to offer us any comments they have about a transaction or anything else about their relationship with Schwab. This does a couple of interesting things. For example, we are able to track the responses back to the service team that helped each customer. And every Schwab team gets composite ratings over the course of a month, quarter, and year that tells them and us how well the customers perceive the service they are delivering.

Third, we use the surveys and our call-monitoring and quality-assurance process to identify exemplary practices as well as problems. Often, we can identify particular phone conversations and pull the tape for review. A supervisor or one of our trainers will sit down with the broker involved, explain what the customer liked or didn't like, and then discuss what they can learn from the critique. Then they will actually listen to the tape with the broker. It's an incredibly powerful experience: Suddenly brokers are hearing how they sound to clients. Any denial about a poor evaluation score has a tendency to melt away then, because the memory of how a call went is never the same as listening to it with a fresh ear.

A summary of all the broker evaluation scores, obviously, translates its way up into management. We also see a sampling of the customer comments, so we can be in better touch with our shortcomings. In addition, a portion of our complaint letters are sent around to top management every month. So, again, we revisit the cases in which customers found us failing, and we learn from them.

Some of our best ideas have come from customers. For years, clients said they wanted to be able to reinvest dividends in their stocks automatically, and in 1992 we designed a system that made this possible. It took a lot of systems analysis, programming, and technical know-how to make this dividend reinvestment service work for virtually any dividend-paying stock. We have 4.8 million accounts, and there are approximately seven thousand stocks on the exchanges. We made it work, and our customers are satisfied. That makes any undertaking worth the effort. Service is one of those intangibles that is hard to measure and, in many cases, hard to make discernible. We're in the business of trying to make our service tangible and marketing the tangibility of that service. It's often in the eye of the customer. It's in the customer experience. Ultimately, customers vote with their wallets, their feet, and their loyalty.

Right now, half our new accounts come from households that are already doing business with Schwab. We're opening more than one million new accounts per year, more than ever before in our history. And existing customers are rewarding us with a greater share of their portfolios, which is extremely gratifying to us.

You can market and advertise and discount all you want, but the rubber meets the road when that call comes in on Sunday afternoon, midnight Tuesday, or in the middle of the busiest trading day of the year from a customer saying, "I need help." Our goal is to be ready for that call. We believe we're on the right track, but our work is never done, and we're never as good as we want to be—or as we're going to be. So we'll just try to do the right things and get better every day.

■ ■ ■

## CHARLES SCHWAB & COMPANY, INC.

### COMPANY PROFILE

| | |
|---|---|
| Business Description | Brokerage |
| Website | www.schwab.com |
| Founded | 1971 |
| Annual Sales | $2.3 billion |
| Net Income | $270 million |
| Employees | 10,400 |
| Products and Selected Services | Discount brokerage services |
| | e.Schwab |
| | Retirement accounts |
| | Schwab TeleBroker services |
| | SchwabLink |

*Wouldn't you love to work in a company where customers flock to your doors and open a hundred thousand new accounts every month on an unsolicited basis? No cold calling, no pressure selling, no sweating, and no hustling to sign up new patrons. The clients simply find you—rather than the other way around.*

*Now imagine having an operation with an annual attrition rate of a mere 6 percent, in an industry where double-digit defection rates are the norm. A place where the president considers solving customer complaints as a turn-around business—and for good reason: Business is up after problems get resolved. And what better evidence of the power of service excellence than this company's growth record—which includes revenues that have mounted more than fivefold during the past seven years (about twice the pace of the investment services industry as a whole) and customer assets that exploded to a sky-high $350 billion in 1997?*

*That's the Schwab story—and testimony to the business wisdom of a value proposition solidly rooted in service excellence.*

*Schwab's ability to attract and keep customers is in my view directly linked to its powerful value proposition. The company takes a stand with the customer that says, "You can depend on us. We demystify investing, and we'll protect you from the rough-and-tumble world out there." In an industry not known for cuddling its customers, where high-pressure tactics seem to be more the norm than the exception, Schwab has carved out a distinct market identity as a gentle company that puts customers and customer relations on a pedestal.*

*Listen to Dave Pottruck's comments about being the custodian of customers' dreams, the core values of the company, and its honest stance—all of which define the business. Then note how these sentiments are translated into hard, actionable, highly efficient operations and management practices. It's a clear fit.*

*I bet that, over the years, Schwab has been tempted to adopt hardball practices and compromise on some of its customer friendliness. I'm also sure that competitors have copied a fair share of Schwab's innovative approaches. In view of that, it's admirable how Schwab has preserved—if not enhanced—its distinct identity over the decades.*

*It wasn't until 1991 that Charles Schwab & Co. began to articulate the firm's core values—and explicitly put on paper what the company stood for in the marketplace. The organization is fortunate in that it has from its inception been guided by a distinct, albeit unwritten, philosophy. The majority of companies I come across have nowhere near the clarity of purpose that characterizes Schwab, and nowhere near their success record either. The lesson: If you're serious about establishing a clear market identity, you and your management team should think through and discuss what it is that sets your business apart from its competitors. There are several techniques I've found useful to stimulate such a discussion, methods that serve as a starting point for creating a shared sense of direction in how to relate to customers.*

- Put your management team in a room with a sheet of paper and ask them to write down in one or two

paragraphs what an outstanding customer testi-
monial for your company would sound like. (The
comments should, of course, go beyond general
praise.)

- Ask the managers to complete this sentence:
  "Customers insist on doing business with us rather
  than competitors such as A and B because we. . . ."
- Ask them to come up with a short "ad" for the business that would fit on a billboard. In a dozen words
  or fewer, what compelling reason could they give a
  prospect to choose this company?
- Describe your company as a person. What personality traits stand out? How do these traits appeal to
  customers?

*Apply these questions to the companies featured in this
book, and you'll get a pretty good idea how to answer
them. Why? Because these organizations have distinctive
value propositions and market identities. Now think about
your own company. Do your people have fuzzy or con-
flicting views of what it is that sets you apart in the marketplace? If so, you know you have your work carved out
for you. By the way, don't rely solely on managers' opinions—get hard data to check management's views against
customers' perceptions.*

*As part of your evaluation, go back to the Schwab story
and note how this company translates its value proposition
into action. Here are some of Schwab's practices that I
would copy in a flash:*

- To keep on track, figure out and remind your people what not to do. Put together your list of fifty of the most troubling policies as they relate to delivering service excellence. Then find a way to change or stop them. (It's like tending a garden; you need to keep weeding if you want to keep it looking nice.)
- Create your own "barrier basher" service enhancement team. Have it identify the scar tissue in your company that causes people to be overly cautious and risk-averse. Then eradicate the procedures rooted in the scar tissue (or bring in fresh people to manage these tasks).
- Replace your procedures books with on-line reference manuals and real-time information that can be updated live with the latest insights, experiences, and facts.

And, finally, how about these nuggets to keep everyone's eyes on the ball:

- Measure your service effectiveness by comparing business results every six months before and after you solve the service problems of customers. That's how Schwab gives meaning to the idea that its customer complaint department is truly a customer turnaround department.
- Link employee incentives to customer service performance. Why didn't we all think about that one?

3

# Lands' End, Inc.

## *Guarantee It Unconditionally*

Throughout much of the twentieth century, mail-order catalogs geared to the general public were not only a popular means of buying goods but also a necessity. Retail catalogs such as the tome issued by Sears, Roebuck & Company and popularly known as the "wish book" helped bridge the vast distances between stores and those consumers located in rural areas who had few chances to see or purchase a company's products. With little regard for market research, Sears could hawk everything from chickens to chain saws because it knew that whoever thumbed through that massive catalog was bound to need something—and usually ordered it.

As highways, both asphalt and electronic, have shrunk the global marketplace in recent years, these all-inclusive, phone-book-thick catalogs have lost their appeal. Television, shopping malls, and now the Internet have connected customers to companies seeking their business, and consumers *can now choose when and how they wish to shop. If they want a chicken or a chain saw, they reach by car or cyberspace a store specializing in that product.*

*Companies seeking mail-order business today create catalogs geared to specific segments of customers. Those companies that meet this marketing challenge position themselves to reap huge gains. The Direct Marketing Association estimates, for instance, that more than 98.5 million Americans—half the adult population—order by mail. And when it comes to meeting the needs of distinctive groups, few catalog companies can match the success of Lands' End, Inc. (www.landsend.com).*

*Founded in Chicago by Gary C. Comer in 1963, Lands' End originally specialized in selling and sometimes manufacturing sailboat supplies. The company mailed its first catalog the following year, and its first color catalog in 1975—the latter dedicating thirty pages to sailing equipment and only two pages to clothing. By 1985, Lands' End was churning out a catalog each month.*

*Today, with over a dozen different specialty catalogs targeting the needs of 25.6 million people on its mailing list, Lands' End derives 95 percent of its revenue from the catalog business. It has built new phone and warehouse operations in the United Kingdom, Japan, and Germany and now distributes its catalogs to over 175 different countries. Forty thousand packages leave its U.S. locations each day. And business is booming. With sales of over $1.1 billion in fiscal 1997—a year in which its earnings rose 67* *percent—the company has surpassed L.L. Bean as the nation's largest apparel catalog.*

*When he founded Lands' End, Gary Comer set up eight guiding principles (discussed below), which underpin the company's standards for customer service. These standards have become something of a mantra: Sell only what you believe in, ship every in-stock order within twenty-four hours, and unconditionally guarantee everything. Comer made sure he and his employees were ready to answer every possible customer question and designed his litera-ture to be equally informative. Once these standards were in place, sales took off. In 1978, with the product focus shifting almost entirely toward garments and apparel, the company moved its rapidly expanding warehouse and phone operations to Dodgeville, Wisconsin—a rural com-munity thirty-eight miles southwest of Madison. It estab-lished a toll-free 800 number that was soon operational twenty-four hours a day, and sales continued to rise.*

*Two decades later, they're still rising.*

## ANN VESPERMAN
### Director of Customer Services

Customer service has always been a huge part of the cul-ture at Lands' End, ever since Gary Comer founded the company. Here we don't just talk about customer focus and doing what's needed to please the customer; we live it every day. That culture grows out of Gary's eight principles for doing business, which everyone at Lands' End knows well. Walk around our headquarters, and you'll see them on office doors, in the warehouse, and at the call center:

1. We do everything we can to make our products better.
2. We price our products fairly and honestly.
3. We accept any return, for any reason, at any time.
4. We ship faster than anyone we know of, shipping items in stock the day after we receive the order.
5. We believe that what is best for our customer is best for all of us.
6. We sell at lower prices by eliminating middlemen, not buying branded merchandise with high protected markups, and placing contracts with cost-conscious, efficient manufacturers.
7. We operate efficiently.
8. We support no fancy emporiums with their high overhead.

## THE LANDS' END WAY OF DOING BUSINESS

If you asked people at most businesses, especially large ones, "What's your company all about?" you would probably get a bunch of different answers. But despite the size of our company, our people are all focused on the vision. And I think that's one of the keys to great customer service: You need to have everybody understand what the vision is and why it's important to follow it. Once you understand the vision, you can live it.

For example, Gary Comer said, "Be good to your people and good to your customers, and the rest will take care of itself." I hear people quote that all the time. And the principles are just as relevant today as when Gary wrote them in 1984.

## Principle #1: Always Seek a Better Way

We're always eager to hear from customers how we can improve our products. Our on-line customer-comment system allows us to record any customer's comments, which can be reviewed daily. Every month we print out a report of these comments about six inches thick and send it to various people throughout the company, as well as to our merchants. We average over fifteen thousand customer comments per month, all of which we study and evaluate before deciding whether to take appropriate action or what to do to better satisfy our customers.

At the request of merchants and product managers, we also survey by telephone a selection of customers for comments on a specific product or service they have recently received. In addition, we forward all written comments to the merchants, although any final changes to product lines are determined by the product team. Merchants also receive a written report of all customer comments relevant to their products.

Sometimes the customer comments lead to major innovations. Our polo shirts, for instance, originally had pockets on them, but in 1996, we revised the shirts and did away with the pockets. Over the next several months we received thousands of comments from people asking us, "Where are you supposed to put your things if you don't have pockets?" So in our next catalog, we brought the pockets back.

Although the change was costly, we believe the benefit of giving our customers the service they expect from us was worth the expense.

We're really never satisfied with a product, no matter how well it does. We had a children's snow boot that was a good seller for us, but in 1996 we completely redesigned it to make it a better product, as our customers requested. Although we had fifteen thousand pairs of the old boot still in stock, we started from scratch. We made the boot more stable, lighter in weight, and more water resistant. We gave it better traction and even made it easier for someone wearing mittens to take it on and off. And when the boot ran in our winter catalogs, we sold more than three times as many pairs as the previous year.

We'll do anything to improve a product—from using finer materials to adding back features or construction details that have been taken out over the years. But one thing we never do: We never reduce the quality of a product to make it cheaper.

### Principle #2: Price Honestly—Always

We refuse to engage in the all-too-common retailing practice of inflating markups to set up a future phony "sale." In fact, we do exactly the opposite. We advertised a line of discounted cotton shirts in our January 1997 catalog under the headline of "Oops! Our Error Becomes Your Gain." We had a lot of extra cotton mesh left over from the previous summer, so we ended up making a bunch of shirts and selling them for less.

One of our vendors sent us dress shirts in the wrong color—chalk white rather than ecru. The shirts we received were distinctly different from what we wanted. So we sold them at $10 cheaper than normal, explaining in our ad copy that there had been an honest "goof" at the vendor site. Whenever mistakes like this occur, we always try to turn them into positive gains for customers.

We don't get into a lot of gimmicks in terms of our pricing, such as bargain-basement sales, giveaways, and buyer's clubs. We believe that giving the best price possible up front for the quality of merchandise that we offer is the way to go with our customers. So while we sell about 90 percent of our merchandise at full price, it's also a fair price. I think our customers can tell the difference and appreciate the honesty.

## Principle #3: Accept Returns for Any Reason

Our products are guaranteed, fair and simple. There is no fine-print or doublespeak in our advertisements, no arguments when you attempt to send something back. We mean exactly what we say: GUARANTEED. PERIOD. This gets to the core of our relationships with customers. We're very careful about how we treat them, how we contact them, how we deal with them when they call. In our surveys, we don't want to intrude on our customers' privacy in any way.

We show our customers respect, and our return policy reflects this attitude: You can return anything—no questions asked. We even take back products that aren't ours, if a customer truly believes it's ours. We respect our customers so much that we never want to question their integrity. It isn't worth upsetting them.

Assuming a product is not defective or altered when it's returned, our people can in most cases get it logged into the system, reinspected, repacked, and back on the shelf the next day. Our outlet stores sell monogrammed, hemmed, and embroidered returns at much reduced prices. And our loss on those few items that are too severely damaged or worn out to resell is a small price to pay for the trust and loyalty that we gain.

We look at our guarantee this way: It's all part of building that relationship of trust with customers. We ask them to buy turtlenecks and Oxford shirts that they have never touched or tried on, but we believe our products are so well made that people will love them. If they don't, we want to do what we can to satisfy them.

"Guaranteed. Period." is a handshake that says "We trust you." And we know it brings us many more sales and friends than it costs us in dollars.

## Principle #4: Get It There Fast

Here's a great story about our shipping policy. One of our customers was at a business meeting on a Saturday when he suddenly realized he needed two hundred purple knit shirts, extra large, to give away to his group. The Lands' End associate who took this call brought in somebody else for help, and the two of them pulled shirts out of the storage area and delivered them by courier before the customer's meeting ended the next day.

Everything ordered from us is processed overnight, picked and packed the next day, then sent out by two-day UPS Air. If you order something today, you'll get it in three days. Even during the holiday season we keep this guarantee. In fact, at the height of the last holiday season the longest time an order was in the house—excepting monograms—was thirty-six hours. Those items with monograms took twelve hours more.

Despite our efficiency, people always need things overnight or sooner. Sometimes our employees go the extra mile to serve them. Late one Friday afternoon, for instance, a customer who had ordered twenty-one shirts for an auto-racing team—twenty for men and one for a woman— called to say the shirts had not yet arrived. The team's first race was the next day, but the shirts had not been shipped because a problem had arisen in color-matching the woman's shirt to those of the men.

Quick thinking saved the day. The young assistant who took the call found a woman's shirt that most closely matched the others, commandeered a colleague to drive her to the Federal Express outlet in Madison, and beat the 6:00 P.M. delivery deadline. The shirts arrived at 10:00 A.M. the next morning, just in time for the race.

During the UPS strike in the summer of 1997, we partnered with the U.S. Postal Service and used its Priority Mail service to make sure that our customers still got their packages relatively quickly—usually in three to five days. From the mini post office we set up at our headquarters, we sent out forty thousand packages a day at the height of the strike. Employees had to work overtime sorting packages manually, but everything got out.

Although customers normally have to pay extra for overnight delivery, during that strike we were offering free delivery because we couldn't promise anything the next day. In those few emergencies where three days wasn't good enough, our own "SWAT" team went to great lengths to make sure customers were satisfied. When one woman, the mother of a bride, called to say she needed blue shoes, our SWAT team FedEx'd her two pairs in two different sizes to make sure she got the right fit.

## Principle #5: Do What Is Best for the Customer

We don't get many irritated customers because whatever we need to do to please them, we do. Our sales and service people are trained to know our products thoroughly and to be friendly and helpful. We pay for every customer's call, and we spend as much time as is needed on each call to make that customer happy.

People enjoy this personal touch. They want to be acknowledged as individuals, and the information we gather for our customer files helps us know each customer thoroughly. Plus, it's a great competitive advantage for us. A lot of companies don't manage their own customer files, but we believe that the more we have at our fingertips, the better we can take care of their requests.

Another reason we excel at customer service is that we give our employees the authority to make decisions. Our frontline people are empowered to take care of the customer however they see fit, right then and there. There is no limit on what an employee can offer a customer.

We have up to four hundred people at each of three main facilities taking calls at one time. The last two weeks before Christmas we have people from different areas of the company help out, a great way for executives and managers to find out more about what it's like on the front lines. And if a person's phone techniques are rusty, there's always an employee on the floor to assist him or her.

We take over a hundred thousand calls daily, but we never rush a customer off the phone. While we're talking to them, we can offer them additional products such as swatches of all the fabrics we sell (excluding leather goods, hand-made quilts, and cashmere). The swatches are free and very useful to anyone trying to figure out a color scheme to match sheets, towels, or table linens with wallpaper, for instance.

We also provide "parts replacement," such as buttons, buckles, belts, and even the changing pads inside diaper bags. If a customer has lost or broken a "part," we send a special request to our parts department, which mails out a new button, buckle, or pad.

Similarly, our Lost Mitten Club will send you a replacement mitten if your child loses one. You can call in anytime during the same season you purchase a pair of Lands' End mittens, and we'll send you a single for half the price of a full pair. We'll even pay for the shipping.

We also take care of hemming and cuffing. In one eight-hour shift our Dodgeville, Wisconsin, distribution facility can hem or cuff twenty thousand pairs of pants. The customers specify length, then choose a regular hem, a cuff, or a military (an "old"-style slanted hem). Everything is free, but you have to wait a day or two extra to get your order.

Customers also appreciate our "specialty shoppers" program, in which some of our customer service staff are trained specifically to handle the most challenging product requests or concerns. If a frontline representative can't handle a customer phone inquiry, the caller is passed on to a specialty shopper in a large room filled with every imaginable Lands' End product. Depending on the request, the specialty shopper can do measurements, match colors, or even describe the texture of fabrics over the phone. Each of our three call centers has such a room where calls are automatically routed (from 6:30 A.M. until midnight) when specialty shoppers at one site are busy.

Often it's the extra attention specialty shoppers provide to customers that saves the day and secures a sale. Over the holidays, for example, we sell Santa hats for dogs. Once a woman with two dogs called in not knowing which size hats to get them. The first representative she talked to suggested she measure the heads of her dogs, but the caller complained that the dogs wouldn't sit still long enough. At this point the representative remembered that one of the specialty shoppers had judged dog shows, so she transferred the customer back to the specialty shopping area. After getting the breed, size, and weight of the dogs, the specialty shopper recommended the best size hats to send—by using her hands to estimate the size while another specialty shopper measured them.

Although 85 percent of our orders are made by phone, we also have twenty-two stores—fifteen outlets and seven "inlets." The outlets are not very fancy but offer tons of discounted overstocked or discontinued merchandise. The inlets are more upscale; for instance, they have an area where you can sit down, have a cup of coffee, and order on a computer from our catalogs. Inlets also have a small selection of our best-sellers (such as turtlenecks and Oxford shirts) at full price—along with "spare parts" such as buttons and belts. The concept behind the inlet stores is to give customers yet another way to get in touch with us in a friendly atmosphere.

In February 1998, we opened our first "Travelers' Inlet" at the Minneapolis–St. Paul International Airport. Designed for people waiting for a flight, the store offers a variety of products and services geared to travelers. Unlike many airport shops, however, there is no markup: All items are priced just as they are in our catalogs.

Maps of two hundred cities, weather updates, currency exchange rates, local hotel, restaurant, and events information, greetings in ten different languages, and complimentary sewing kits are just a few of the offerings available at the store, which will ship any purchased items to your destination or home. If you decide to buy a new piece of luggage from us, you can repack right in the store and arrange to have your old bag donated to a local charity. There are free crayons, coloring books, and travel journals for the kids, and interactive kiosks posted outside the store where people can log on to the Internet and order from the Lands' End Website twenty-four hours a day. So if you're stranded just before Christmas Eve, you can order that last-minute gift.

## Principle #6: Work Directly with Manufacturers

While vendor manufacturers handle the actual production of goods, our merchandising team for each product does the design, picks out the fabric, and develops construction and quality standards. The merchandiser-vendor relationship is one of constant communication. We call ourselves "direct merchants" rather than "mail-order marketers" because we work with our vendors and customers to make sure that what ends up in our catalog is the best.

Our specialty shoppers and merchandisers work together to put on a two-hour forum each product season called "For Your Information (FYI)." Merchandisers and customer sales staffs bring in samples of new products for that season, as well as discuss current products. With feedback from customer service representatives and supervisors, these forums give us a chance to have honest and profitable discussion about these products.

Each month we invite some merchants to listen to customer phone calls during a scheduled "talk time," then discuss the calls with Lands' End representatives. And at least once a quarter, merchants attend sessions when their products are on the agenda to be discussed by selected customer service staff in "open forum" sessions.

Product ideas often result from these close relationships. In the March 1998 Lands' End catalog, we introduced larger sizes in many of our women's clothes (sizes

18W–26W) and accessories, primarily because our sales representatives had heard from thousands of customers desiring full-figured items. We make sure such ideas are heard—and acted upon.

Having such close alliances with our vendors also allows us to offer special values to our customers. A few years back, a Lands' End mill ordered yarn for a job that didn't materialize as hoped. The yarn was taking up needed storage space on mill shelves until product manager Christopher Merritt devised a solution. "Remember that idea for a mock-T that I had a while back?" he asked the mill operators. "If you could knit it for the right price, we could make that yarn disappear." The resulting product, a 100 percent cotton jersey that could be worn year-round, was ready for the January 1997 catalog at a discounted price of $39. The headline, as usual, told the story: "How a tough storage problem turned into a sweet deal for you."

## Principle #7: Train for Efficiency

Our employees are extremely knowledgeable because we make a big commitment to training them. I think it's one thing to talk about our philosophy with people, but it's actually putting that philosophy into practice that helps the most. When you go through the training and you're around people who do it every day, you're influenced in a positive manner. You see that people are living what they're talking about, and you become a part of that mind-set.

Each customer service representative we hire goes through an initial seventy-hour training class, divided into product training and systems training. They first learn the history and culture of Lands' End—who our customers are, why they are important to us, and how we treat them. Next comes a study of the order-entry system, including hands-on training. Finally, new hires learn every last detail about how we make our products, how we source the fabric, and how we deal with vendors. We omit nothing. They not only understand the product's design and manufacturing but come to know the product itself.

After this initial seventy hours of instruction, we begin "continuous training," three-hour sessions each month to update employees on new products appearing in the catalogs, system changes, or anything else we need to share with them. As we add new products to catalogs and make system changes that affect what's done on the front line, it's important that everyone keep up-to-date with the latest revisions.

We don't offer sales incentive plans to our salespeople who take calls on the floor. Our mission here is to take care of the customer. If a customer wants something and it's back-ordered or no longer available, we have alternate products to offer. We train people to say, "We don't have X, but we do have Z. Would you be interested?" Most call-center operations measure talk time, number of calls per hour, and so on. We know what our talk time is, but that isn't a performance statistic by which we manage customer representatives. We measure our success by whether our customers are satisfied—and whether they stay with us.

We also offer optional job sharing. This is a great vehicle for the company and its workers. We have people here in customer sales who are also cross-trained in our customer service department.

We like to think of our customer service people as our second tier of support. If there's a major problem that can't be handled by the frontline representative, the call is transferred to customer service. We have a number of people who are knowledgeable in both of those jobs and could also be trained in other areas such as manufacturing. The concept of job sharing makes great sense; the more employees learn about the company as a whole, the better they understand the different systems. And with this knowledge, they can do their jobs better.

## Principle #8: Find the Right Place to Do Your Best Work

People laugh when I tell them Lands' End is located in the middle of a forty-acre cornfield. But there's a reason for it. I think that part of Gary Comer's master plan when he came to Dodgeville was to find a midwestern town with down-to-earth people who had a strong work ethic. He knew that if he hired from this base, he would be hiring people dedicated to Lands' End.

He was right on the mark. Lands' End has been good to the community, and the community has been good to the company. The people in Dodgeville really believe in us. A lot of people may think the work ethic changes little from one organization to another, but these are committed people who work here.

A lot of people ask if we train our people to be nice. But you can't train people to be genuinely friendly. We're very lucky at Lands' End to have such employees, about 90 percent of whom live in or around Dodgeville, and that's part of what makes our customer service operation unique. And that's why we've also located all three of our call centers—one here at headquarters and two in smaller communities—within an hour of downtown Dodgeville.

As a result of our strong ties to the community, a lot of families in Dodgeville and the surrounding areas have more than one family member working here. This is important to us, especially at Christmastime when we need to have close to eight thousand employees at work throughout the world. About 70 percent of the employees we get to come work here at Christmas are referrals—many of them family members, neighbors, and friends of regular workers. During the rest of the year we have about 5,400 employees, but during the holiday season we do 40 percent of our annual business in three months and need the extra help.

We start training our seasonal employees early enough so that we can put everyone through the same seventy hours of training—even the people who are only going to be here for three months. And we get a lot of returnees. Thirty percent of our seasonal workers in 1997 were rehires. Homemakers and farmers work here in their off-season to make some extra money for the holidays. Some of our other temps are retirees who do everything from wrap gift boxes to take phone calls, and we also have a lot of college students working in our warehouse. They arrive daily by bus from the University of Wisconsin–Platteville forty miles away.

So although our company has gone through many changes in both the products it sells and the way it reaches customers, the original ideals and principles Gary put forth some thirty-five years ago still apply. We still seek to make the best possible product, sell it at the fairest price we can, and get it to our customers as quickly as possible. We continue to train for excellence, work closely with our manufacturers, and operate as efficiently as we can. And, of course, we still stand by everything we sell with our no-questions-asked guarantee.

*Lands' End catalogs do far more than let customers know what the company has for sale. With humorous, full-length features such as "The Story of a Shirt" and informative notes such as "How much down do we put in our winter jackets—and why?" the catalogs often read more like encyclopedias of fabric facts and company history than descriptions of merchandise. In fact, people look forward to reading the Lands' End catalog.*

*This friendly, instructive approach is cited by customers as a major reason they believe the company cares so much about its products—and the people who buy them. Combined with its reasonable prices and its liberal "Guaranteed. Period." return policy, the Lands' End strategy helps eliminate the stigma people often associate with mail-order catalogs as being a risky way to shop. Certainly a company that lets you know it uses the fleece of four*

*cashmere goats found in inner Mongolia to make each*
*cashmere sweater wants to win your confidence and trust.*

## MICHAEL P. ATKIN
### Vice President and Director of Marketing

I think the biggest challenge that anybody in our business has is the catalog itself. Obviously we have to offer great products. Our customers expect that of us. And we have to offer great service, because they expect that too. But where the rubber meets the road is when you open your mailbox and you've got seven inches of junk mail along with a Lands' End catalog. The challenge for us is to make that Lands' End catalog a wonderful thing that you look forward to getting. That takes a lot of effort from a lot of creative people.

We differ from most other companies in the way we construct our catalogs. If you read the pages where we talk about products, I think you'll see that everything we're doing there is geared to relating in a simple, no-nonsense way what the benefit of that product is to the customer. Even though we take a lot of words to do it—more than probably anybody else uses—those words are all focused on helping the customer decide, "Would this be a product I would want?" and "What are some of the things it offers that would be helpful to me?"

You may be reading a few more words in our catalogs, but in the end I think you're probably spending less time actually deciding on a product because you're more certain by the time you're finished reading that "Yes, this is something I would really like," or "No, this is not something

I'm interested in." With a mailing list of 25.6 million customers, we're always trying to segment people so we know who wants what products. We even send several different catalogs to the same house depending on who lives there.

## A TEAM ON TARGET

Our creative department is all in-house. The writers and art directors actually sit with the product teams, the merchandisers, and the inventory people. They are surrounded by the products, so they know everything about the last stitch on the turtleneck as soon as the product manager does. The only freelance writing we use is for the additional editorial stories. Everything else is done here by our own people.

It's the creative team working in conjunction with our product people that decides whether or not we give customers some interesting tidbit such as how we measure the amount of goose down we put in our parkas. It's really the same thing you would find in an advertising agency. You've got the guy who really understands the customer, the product, and what the company adds to the mix for the customer's benefit. Then you've got the creative team that needs to find a way to phrase that in terms the customer will understand. It's that pairing of the expert who knows the product with the people who know how to bring out the benefits creatively that makes the process so fascinating to watch.

## ON THE HUNT

The most powerful way we have of attracting new customers is word of mouth. If your neighbor receives our catalog, he or she can request a catalog subscription (three issues) for you, or you yourself can call in for one. We also have an advertising campaign we run in some select magazines and on cable TV with a phone number for you to call in. Then there are opportunities to obtain certain lists of customers to target specifically.

We aren't a company that does a lot of focus groups or concept testing, then goes out and tries to create a product. The best research we have is the product itself. Of course, we're not always sure what people like. We really started doing catalog editorials back in 1984–1985, not knowing whether they would work but just believing that this was the kind of thing that might be fun for our customers to have as part of their catalog experience. Once we started running them, we began getting positive comments such as "Hey, this is great! Do more of it." It really starts with a belief that we're offering more than just pictures and price.

How do we know whether our customers want to read a story by Charles Osgood in the catalog? We depend on what they tell us. Every operator here can record customer comments as they come in over the phone. Looking at all of this feedback, we get a lot of positive reinforcement for the articles, features, crossword puzzles, and the other features we put into our catalogs. So we keep it up.

## Something for Everyone

Our "Kids" catalog goes back about ten years to the point at which we noticed that a large number of our customers had children. We naturally began thinking about offering clothing for the kids. When we studied the market, we realized that a lot of children's clothing was made cheaply—not to last but to wear out quickly. Nobody expected much of it. We asked ourselves, "What could Lands' End bring to our customers that would be both a real benefit for them and a major difference from what's out there now?"

It was clear what we needed: better quality clothes for kids. So we vowed to make our children's apparel as good as Lands' End adult clothing. This strategy helped make our products unique. We gave it a shot, and once we got the initial favorable response, we let the product lines grow from there.

Now we've focused all of our lines on more tailored clothing. We have our "Beyond Buttondowns" business wear catalog, which includes business shirts, suits and "suit separates," ties, shoes, and anything else men wear to work. We also have a women's catalog called "First-Person Singular," which really does the same thing for women. And we have the "Coming Home" catalog that's geared to household items such as linens and towels.

The case of "Beyond Buttondowns" is identical to what we did with the Kids catalog. We believe you shouldn't have to pay $1,000 to get a great suit, so one advantage we offer is "suit separates." You can measure yourself and get the exact pair of pants you want, then measure yourself again to get the exact jacket you want. We'll even send you a tape measure and instructions to teach you how to give us your measurements.

We offer full suits, but the idea is that not everybody is

made to look like Superman. In fact, a lot of us have coats and pants as wrinkled and ill-fitting as Clark Kent's wardrobe. Everybody has a slightly different body shape, so we strive to give customers more flexibility in their choices of clothes. This kind of service would be hard to find outside Lands' End unless you went to a tailor and had a suit custom-made. And even though you purchase the jacket and pants separately, we're very careful to make sure that the fabric, the patterns, and everything else blend together so you don't look as if you are mixing pieces from two different suits.

## The Right People for the Job

We work long and hard to make sure every item in our catalogs meets Lands' End strict standards for excellence. That starts with our product managers, all of whom are true experts in their product lines. They live and breathe their products. If they have to go to Spain and Portugal four times a year to meet with people at the mill, that's what they do. They read every single letter and customer comment that comes in concerning their products. We even have customers sending us competitors' products, saying, "I wish you'd put this in your catalog" or "Look at this."

But while our product managers digest everything, they don't just react with some sort of compromise. They come at it with an expert's eye, to figure out what makes a particular product work and what it needs to do. From there, they consider if there is something we could do to make it better—more functional, lighter, warmer, or cooler. They don't create new products merely for the sake of change.

It's important that the product managers always be in touch with the manufacturer. It's a real engineering process. Because we work with large quantities, we need lead time, and we have to be sure that a product, if changed, still meets three criteria: It benefits the customer; the customer will be able to read about it in the catalog and understand it easily; and it won't result in a lot of excess inventory. All three elements must be considered.

Of course, it's tough to decide exactly what all your customers are going to want from a few samples. But I think you have to use your judgment. We pay our product people to make judgments about what is and what isn't an improvement.

## PRACTICE MAKES PERFECT

I don't want to give you the impression we don't do any focus groups. We do some. But there are a number of us here who have worked in advertising, and we've seen the overreliance and misuse of focus groups. You really have to be careful, I think, of getting eight or nine people in a room and making a lot of assumptions about whether they're able to tell you what you really need to know. But when you go about them the right way, focus groups can be very helpful.

For example, we've had panels of Lands' End customers that we've brought together to help us improve products. In early 1996, when we were working on ways to achieve better fit in women's jeans, we asked a group to try on a lot of jeans, then modified the fit based on their reactions. We wound up actually having a photo shoot here in our gym where our customers modeled the jeans. The whole thing went so well, the pictures eventually appeared in our catalog. So it's more than a focus group. We're really trying to look at customers every which way in an attempt to understand how they feel about our clothing.

We also work with customers on "wear testing." For example, we wanted to come out with a new line of wheeled luggage in 1996. Working with three airlines, we created prototypes that flight attendants from Midwest Express, United, and Northwest Airlines could use. Flight attendants probably wheel more luggage through airports than anybody else, so we were setting up a torture test for the luggage.

By the end of the test, we knew a lot more about how we should make the luggage. For one thing, we saw the damage done to the wheels and realized we needed to switch to bigger wheels such as the ones used for in-line skates. We figured they would be able to handle all the pits and cracks luggage has to roll over. We also widened the track on the wheels so that the bags wouldn't tip over.

We talked to the flight attendants, who told us when they had trouble rolling the pieces across the floor or getting them on planes. They also answered a lot of questions for us: Did the luggage fit in the overhead compartment? Did it tip over? Was the retracting handle at the right height? Was it convenient to reach? These are all issues you want answered before customers start buying a product.

We ask our employees and their families to help us out with wear-testing products as well. Employees take items home to use in real-life situations, and we get some great feedback that way. In fact, employees are probably some of our best long-term customers.

## KNOWING WHAT INNOVATIONS TO MAKE— AND WHEN

If you went back and looked at a Lands' End catalog from ten years ago and compared it with one from today, I think you would see the identical philosophy in terms of product quality and service philosophy. The products, of course, have changed: For example, outerwear ten years ago meant a heavy parka with all the insulation built into one garment; now people mix and match apparel, often wearing several layers. Although many product concepts have changed, however, the emphasis on quality and service stays the same.

We try to stay ahead of the current level of customer service demands. Some years ago we were the first major catalog company to send out a catalog offering a toll-free phone service—which we started in 1978 and expanded to a twenty-four-hour service two years later. Everybody in our industry thought that was crazy. They told us we would never get the money back that we invested. But it turned out that this service was something the customers really appreciated and wanted. Then, in 1994, we went to two-day delivery using UPS at no premium charge because we felt our busy customers would appreciate it. There have been a lot of other things that we've added over the years, both as a result of ideas brought up by people here or from customers who call in asking for a change.

There is no question that we have stiffer competition than ever before. There are a lot more companies competing for customers, and more catalogs in the mailbox each week, particularly at holiday time. It's a growing challenge, and that's what makes it fun to come to work here. You've always got things going on, and you're always trying to be as good as you can be.

## MICHAEL J. SMITH
### President, Lands' End

We're much bigger than we were when I came here fifteen years ago as a college intern. There are a lot of things that have physically changed about the company. But I think we've managed to hold on to those key elements that really make Lands' End special. Things like our philosophy, people, camaraderie, customer service focus, and emphasis on quality. Those are the things I spend a lot of time thinking about as I focus on the future—making sure those values never change.

## WHO ELSE BUT LANDS' END?

I see customer service as one of the foundations of our business. If you look at what we stand for in the marketplace, product quality and customer service are probably the two primary things you'll find. Then underlying both of those factors is a fun, innovative approach to the business. I like to say that we're willing to try new things, take chances, and encourage people. We want to make people say, "Who else but Lands' End would do something like that?" Simply put, customer service is a critical part of who we are and our position in the marketplace.

## HIRE RIGHT, TREAT RIGHT

Gary Comer's beliefs about how you should treat customers and employees remain in place today, and they still come from the top. The wrong people established in positions of higher management can change the entire culture and atmosphere of your company.

When I was interviewing people for management jobs, one key post I found very difficult to fill was that of CFO/chief administrator. Many people normally associated with that position are very hard-nosed, bottom-line kind of leaders—which runs counter to the culture we have here. Obviously, there is a certain amount of control inherent in that job. But we also need someone who understands our culture. I told our interviewers, "We want the kind of person who will stop when they see someone on the side of the road and offer a hand." If we're hiring people that fit that description, it's a lot easier to maintain our culture as we grow.

There is a place for hard-nosed business criteria without having to sacrifice a strong customer service culture. I think what you have to do is take the long-term view: If we satisfy the customer, the business is also going to be healthy. That's what I stress. If you take that view, I think you'll find a lot fewer inconsistencies between customer service and financial performance.

We really don't find it all that difficult to maintain this philosophy of customer service. A big reason is the contact and communication we have throughout the company. The employees on the front line are constantly hearing from a number of people—from me to other senior executives to their managers to their supervisors—that the customer comes first. We're always reinforcing that with incentives, with rewards, and with pats on the back. When issues come up, our first response is always "How does this affect the customer?" or "What's the customer going to think of this?" If you get into the habit of doing that, it's not so difficult to continue doing it.

## There's No Bottom Line on Customer Service

We keep an eye on what other companies are doing with regard to customers, but we're not fanatical about it. Internally, we always try to be very respectful of the competition. Of course, we're on top of who the competition is and what they're doing, but we don't spend a lot of time worrying about it. I want to see most of our efforts focused on the future and the customer, not the competition. I want other people to spend their time watching us rather than vice versa.

We're always asking questions of ourselves. What can we do that nobody else out there is doing? For our customers, a big part of the buying process is making things easier for them and giving them what they can get excited about. That's really what we're after when we look at implementing a product or service. We think our customers would think it's neat.

For example, when we sponsored Hodding Carter on his Viking ship voyage during the summer of 1997, a lot of people thought we were absolutely crazy. People asked me, "Is this part of some elaborate marketing scheme?" You know what, it was as simple as this: We thought our customers would be interested in it. We thought it was a neat idea, so we did it. Our readers and Internet users also loved it. We tracked the progress of Carter's team as it traveled from Greenland to Newfoundland wearing Lands' End clothing and riding in a man-powered replica of an authentic Viking ship (the trip commemorated Leif Eriksson's journey along a similar path a thousand years ago), and gave updates in our catalogs and daily on our Website.

Customers enjoyed sharing in the adventure so much, we followed it up by sponsoring Bill Cotter and his sixteen Alaskan huskies as they trained for and competed in the 1,100-mile Iditarod Trail Sled Dog Race across Alaska in March 1998. Visitors to our site could track the Cotter team's progress throughout the race and ask real-time questions of reporters Joe Runyan and Lisa Mullen—who followed Bill and his dogs each step of the way. Lisa, in fact, is a Lands' End employee.

Although I can't spell out ROI to the satisfaction of every accountant, we do have ways for tracking customer satisfaction and retention. We know that the net effect of everything we did last year, including sponsoring the Carter team, is working. So what we do is say, "Okay, great, we're going to build on that." And our litmus test, so to speak, is simply whether it's going to be worth it to the customer. We know what it's costing us. But are customers going to get excited enough so that we feel the money is justifiably spent? I know for a fact that there are some things we do that never pay. But I don't know which ones until our customers speak up—and they always do.

## THE ROLE OF TECHNOLOGY

For the last twenty-five years, technology has been absolutely critical to our business. When computers first came on the scene, that's really what allowed us—and the catalog industry in general—to grow during the 1980s. Today we try to use technology to focus on the question of what else we can do for customers. How can we make it easier for them to shop? How can we get them more excited about it? We're always looking for what's out there, but we're also careful not to go overboard. I think you can get carried away with technology. You can run into the problem of always needing to have the latest and best technology, which turns out to also be the most expensive. You have to be careful.

The Internet, of course, is a completely new customer channel for us. It's rapidly changing and in many ways expanding the field, and we're still learning about it. What can this medium allow us to do that we can't do with the print catalog, or that we can't do through a retail store?

How can we utilize the unique strengths of this particular technology to benefit our customers?

The Internet is already changing the way a lot of people shop. It's going to take a while to impact everyone because most companies right now are still viewing the Internet as just a new place to slap up something they were doing somewhere else. But the strengths and capabilities of the medium are such that we are able to do things that we simply could not do before. I expect to see dramatic improvements over the next five or ten years as technology becomes more integrated into both our catalog and retail business.

Overall, I don't think anyone knows for sure where things are going to end up with regard to the Internet. So we have to be flexible and remain focused on the customer and customer behavior, because there is no way to know how it will evolve. But there are things about people that haven't changed in years. And we try to focus on that and figure out what people will be comfortable using, what they are going to want and need. That helps to demystify and clarify things a little bit on the technology front.

## WHERE ARE WE HEADED?

Customers are more demanding today than they were five years ago, and competition is a big driver. Obviously, if you've been around a few years and you're the only game in town and people need your product, they're going to come and buy it from you. But if they have ten places to buy it from, they're going to go to whoever is treating them best. When product quality is similar, it's customer service that tips the scale in your favor.

In terms of customer service, I wish for many things. Here's one idea. When we print up and send out a catalog, it's out there forever. We develop all of our products ourselves, so we have very long product lead times. Unfortunately, because forecasting is not a science, we run out of some products or they don't meet our quality standards. Then we disappoint customers who see those products in the guide and want them. This is one of the biggest frustrations we have.

My vision is to at some point have essentially a virtual catalog that you can take with you wherever you go. We can change it by the minute if we want, or by the day, or whatever. The key is that the changes will be based both on what we have in stock and what the customer wants. There is no paper involved, so we can eliminate all of the expense and waste of catalogs. We will be able to put exactly what the customers want directly in front of them—when they want it.

Now *that's* customer service.

■■■

## LANDS' END, INC.

## COMPANY PROFILE

| | |
|---|---|
| Business Description | Retail catalog |
| Website | www.landsend.com |
| Founded | 1963 |
| Annual Sales | $1.26 billion |
| Net Income | $51 million |

| Employees | 8,400 |
|-----------|-------|
| Products | Accessories |
| | Children's clothing and apparel |
| | Domestic products |
| | Holiday gifts |
| | Men's clothing and apparel |
| | Soft luggage |
| | Women's clothing and apparel |

*I must admit, Lands' End has puzzled me for some time. Nothing seems to perturb this company, nothing seems to get it off balance. Try putting it to the test and call its customer service department at peak hours during the busiest season, as I did just before the holidays last year. I bet you won't get forever-put-on-hold, frazzled operators on the phone. Most likely, you'll be connected instantly to the most empathetic person who seems to have all the time in the world to help you. "Sure, sir, you would like to order a Christmas stocking? No problem, sir. And you would like to have it monogrammed with only five days to go before the big day? No problem, sir. We'll take care of it, sir. Thank you for choosing Lands' End."*

*Where do they find people like that? How do they train them so well? How do they manage to fulfill a last-minute customized order and get it in your hands an unbelievable two days later? How do they manage to stay on top of their highly competitive industry? Talking to Lands' End's managers didn't get me the answers I was looking for. I was expecting to discover some intricate, grand strategy behind the company's enduring success. President Michael Smith told me there wasn't one, and I must confess I wasn't able to discern it. The real secret of Lands' End, I think, is that it is has perfected simplicity for thirty-five years straight. Its strength, to paraphrase Peter Drucker, is to "make things look easy that others are sweating."*

*No wonder the Lands' End people know what they're doing. Lands' End seems to be operating on a different timeline from its competition. During the 1980s, some bright consumer marketers hit on the idea that offering everyday-low-prices instead of promotion-riddled price deals would be a superb way to attract customers. Never mind that Lands' End's principle #2 ("fair and honest pricing") embraced that thinking many years earlier. During the 1990s, a big wave of reengineering and restructuring took place at many organizations. One of the most frequent goals: enhance customer service operations by designing everything to be done simply and quickly—with a minimum of frills. Think about it. That's exactly how Lands' End was set up from day one.*

*Anyone wanting to design an ideal foundation on which to build a superb customer service operation would be wise to incorporate many of the practices in place at Lands' End. Here are some that are effective not only because they preempt the need for customer service, but also because they clear the way for rapid handling of any customer-related activity:*

***Produce quality products.*** *Constantly improve them. Torture-test them. Work with your suppliers to make your* products unsurpassed in quality. Take them back if customers don't like them, then make sure you correct any problems so similar returns don't happen again. And keep working at it.

**Coach your customers so they choose and use your products appropriately.** Use advertising, promotional materials, catalogs, and whatever other means necessary to educate them on what to expect. View your marketing and communications departments as an extension of your customer service.

**Learn from your customers—with a vengeance.** Put in place streamlined processes to extract lessons from customer service calls, letters, and other experiences. Make sure customer feedback and input (both positive and critical) is disseminated widely across the organization and doesn't simply stop at the desks of frontline providers. Ensure your employees are truly in touch with customers, especially when they don't see these customers face-to-face.

**Earn the trust of customers.** Give them the benefit of the doubt. Put their interests ahead of yours. Tolerate their foibles. Treat them the way you would like to be treated, and don't wait until they ask for something before giving it to them. (Remember how Lands' End initiated 1-800 calls and two-day delivery at no extra charge?)

Relentlessly strive for simplicity of design and operations.

Develop your own equivalent of Lands' End's eight principles. Then live them.

Finally, if you have to build a service excellence business from the ground up, try to locate it in a place like Dodgeville, Wisconsin.

# 4

# American Express Company

*Make Membership a Privilege*

**M**embership in American Express (www.american-express.com) may, indeed, have its privileges, but customers have come to think of extraordinary service as their right. That's because the nearly 150-year-old firm scrupulously cultivates its image as the premier provider of travel and financial services, and in so doing, has made security, prestige, and service synonymous with the name American Express. A value proposition built around the delivery of world-class service has consistently been the foundation for every American Express product and service.

Consistency has not been the rule in the credit industry as a whole, however. Recent years have witnessed dramatic change and greatly intensified competition, largely brought about by technological advancements. ATM machines now dot the landscape worldwide, making it possible to withdraw cash from bank accounts at any time of the day or *night. Competitors such as Visa and MasterCard are no longer the poor relations of the credit industry, having gained universal acceptance. And debit cards have become the plastic alternative to personal checks—a cashless way to pay.*

*Amid this fast and furious pace of change, American Express has sometimes stumbled—most notably with debt problems when it first introduced its Optima credit card and a sharp decline in the number of cardholders and participating merchants in the early 1990s. High service charges drove away merchants, while competition from no-annual-fee credit cards appealed to customers reluctant to pay $55 a year for the famous piece of green plastic.*

*A turnaround quietly began to take shape in 1993, however, when Harvey Golub took over as chief executive officer. Having shed businesses without a close strategic fit to the company's core services—such as Shearson Lehman and some of its magazines—the company now concentrates on charge and credit cards, travel, and financial services. In making these moves, Golub has returned American Express to a premier position among U.S. corporations. Record earnings in 1997, including a net income of $1.99 billion (up 14 percent over 1996), evidence the magnitude of recovery, as do the company's membership rolls: As of mid-1997, American Express had roared back with a list of cardholders totaling some 42.7 million people worldwide, who spent $209 billion in 1997.*

*Now Golub is pushing innovation, with numerous new*

card products targeted to specific market segments. The plan appears to be working. During the past two years, the company introduced more new cards than it had in the prior ten.

For the future, an increased global presence seems to be the rallying cry. Golub wants foreign operations to contribute half the company's earnings by 2005. It has already entered into deals with more than a score of bank partners overseas to issue American Express charge and credit cards, and it is courting additional bank clients who see potential profit in shifting to the American Express network. For one thing, brand strength and service features still entice millions of consumers to pay anywhere from $55 to $300 a year for many of the American Express cards. For another, a higher American Express merchants' fee—although lower than it was a few years back—could translate into more money for the bank partners than they can get from rivals Visa and MasterCard.

On the home front, American Express is trying to project a less highbrow, more versatile image in an effort to get customers to think of using their cards for all manner of purchases, not just travel and luxury items. New vendors range from gas stations to discount stores, with new president and heir apparent Kenneth Chenault under the belief that the brand's important characteristics of security and service won't be compromised by making a customer's day-to-day life easier. As he explains it, "If our customer wants to use the American Express card at a hot dog stand, we want to be there."

## STEVEN GRANT

Executive Vice President, Service Delivery
American Express Travel Related Services Company, Inc

# World-Class Service: The Cornerstone of Value

A culture built around personalized service is what sets us apart from our competitors. It's a culture that treats each customer as an individual and recognizes the value that each brings to our company.

Here's an example of what I mean. A few years back, one of our American Express employees, Sarita in New Delhi, received a fax from a Gold Cardmember who was on holiday with his family in Leh, a Himalayan village, and was almost completely out of funds. He needed help with travel arrangements and access to emergency cash.

Sarita sprang into action. She first arranged the family's travel accommodations, then started searching for a way to deliver the money—not an easy task since Leh doesn't have any travel offices. Sarita called John, another employee in the New Delhi Travel operation, and explained the cardmember's dilemma. John, in turn, contacted his brother, a pilot in the Indian army stationed close to Leh. The brother managed to deliver the funds by flying to Leh in a military helicopter.

Although Sarita and John were formally recognized by American Express as two of its "Great Performers" for 1996, extraordinary service on behalf of a customer is not all that uncommon at our company. True, few acts of service include military helicopter pilots, but countless employees go to great lengths each day to place the interests of customers first and to make them feel special—and secure—when they use American Express.

## INDIVIDUALIZING THE CUSTOMER EXPERIENCE

Such stories illustrate the dramatic turns life can take when a company's value proposition is based on meeting the individual needs of more than forty-two million customers twenty-four hours a day, seven days a week. We consistently try to innovate our service delivery, and we consider ourselves to be the best in the financial services industry. Our ability to differentiate that service while making sure that our products meet the very high expectations of our customers is key to our success.

We have expanded on a number of different market fronts in the past few years, and the cornerstone of all these new products has been the delivery of world-class service. Our customers have very high expectations of us, so we build all our products around a basic concept of being the world's most respected service brand. We are committed to delivering what our discriminating customers expect.

## ADJUSTING TO CUSTOMER PATTERNS

One of the most classic examples of individualization is the no preset spending limit on our charge cards. "No preset spending limit" means that the limit is not set in advance as for a typical credit card that gives a line of credit up to $5,000.

We actually look at the individual customer's needs, spending patterns, ability to pay, and up-to-date payment history to adjust spending thresholds on a transaction-by-transaction basis. Every time customers make a purchase, we recalibrate our system to reflect what they have spent, what they typically spend, and what their current payment status is.

A key reason many people like our charge cards is that they like the freedom of spending what they need to spend and the financial discipline of paying in full at the end of the month—although we also have flexible payment options on our charge cards, which I'll talk more about later. By customizing our spending limits, we're able to accommodate a range of lifestyles: People who spend anywhere from $100,000 to $1 million a year can be accommodated just as readily as people who spend $5,000 to $10,000 per year. As long as they fulfill our financial criteria, such as paying on time, we're able to meet their expectations.

## THE ROLE OF TECHNOLOGY

In the early 1990s, when we first introduced the Optima card, we had trouble matching the right credit lines with the right customer. Now, using our extensive database of information, we can better match card options, lines of credit, interest rates, and more for each of our customers. We also have special purchase accounts that give customers more payment flexibility. For example, charge cardmembers with those accounts can extend payments on larger purchases, such as travel or furniture. Our objective is to make customer service seamless and relevant to each customer by leveraging our database and learning from all our interactions with customers.

## KNOWING THE CUSTOMER

To know our customers better as individuals, we leverage information in three key areas: servicing, product marketing and usage, and managing credit risk. The risk management information, of course, defines appropriate lending levels for individual customers based on their credit histories and income levels. The service information tells the company how and when customers actually use its products or services and which aspects customers appreciate most. The marketing information identifies purchasing patterns, attitudes, and values. It is in the service and marketing areas that American Express far outshines its rivals.

For example, we now call our billing statement a customer reward system relationship statement. New technology has allowed us to revolutionize the way we do billing in order to improve both customer service and merchandising. By looking at each customer's habits and by working with merchants who also want to build customer loyalty, we can give each cardmember rewards on his or her monthly statement that match that person's lifestyle.

We're getting down to the customer level, saying, "Here are things we know this customer is likely to be interested in, based, in part, on past history of spending. Let's make sure that we offer this person additional opportunities to get value-added offers and rewards." It's a very customized approach.

For this program, which is called CustomExtras, American Express works with particular merchants to develop offers for specific customers that both reward patronage and build loyalty to each merchant's store. CustomExtras appear on a customer's statement as messages beside relevant transactions. A message may read, "We know you shopped at XYZ Department Store last month. Shop there three more times, and you will get 20 percent off." If the merchant wants to boost sales in the menswear department, the offer could be tailored as such and sent to customers likely to take advantage of it. The second time the customer shops at the store, the billing statement reminds her that only two more visits will result in a reward.

Both the merchant and the customer benefit from this program. Merchants can cut through marketing clutter by reaching an audience that is most likely to take advantage of an offer. Similarly, customers can benefit from offers quite relevant to the way they shop and live. And one of the best things about CustomExtras is that it takes advantage of the fact that our bills have a 100 percent "open rate." They are among the few pieces of business-related mail that is read by virtually 100 percent of their audience.

## More Groups Rate Personal Treatment

We go to great lengths to understand and respond to the needs of individual customers. Witness the multiple ways in which we develop products and services that meet the needs of specific customer segments.

For example, we have different cards for senior members,

college students, and golf enthusiasts. For senior members, we provide a special values page with offers that would be attractive to them, such as cruises, shopping, dining, and other products or services geared to their group. College students, meanwhile, receive a different page that might feature deals on airfares, CDs, and long-distance calling. And as for the golfers, special privileges include advance tee-time reservations at over 140 U.S. golf courses, as well as access to all-inclusive golf travel packages and rewards options ranging from a Big Bertha putter to a full set of clubs.

But American Express market differentiation doesn't stop there. Another group of cards offer rewards. These include enrolling charge cards in the Membership Rewards Program and cobranded cards, including the Delta SkyMiles Card and the Hilton Optima Card. Cardholders can earn free air travel, hotel stays, exotic cruises and vacations, gourmet food, fashion, electronics, and more—just for making everyday purchases with these cards. Customers and potential customers can apply for these programs and other cards on our Website at www.americanexpress.com, where they can also review their accounts, pay their bills, and check out special travel deals.

## HIRING THE RIGHT PEOPLE
American Express's extensive use of technology enables employees to concentrate on building stronger relationships with customers. We believe that hiring the right kinds of employees is critical to providing the American Express brand of customer service.

A fairly extensive set of tests and interviews take place during the hiring process, and all are based on competency models. What kind of service orientation does a person have? What is going to be the person's readiness to try to solve customer problems? Once hired, new service-center employees receive five weeks of full-time classroom training. Then, depending on the function, we offer one to three months of on-the-job training. I think this latter element is unique in two areas.

Floor walkers, or assist people, are assigned to help representatives at our telephone service center so that these new hires will actually work with an experienced person during the on-the-job training period. One experienced person is assigned to help four new representatives. This veteran provides side-by-side coaching and feedback as the rookies take calls. This type of intensive support on the floor gets new customer service representatives up the learning curve and makes sure that they're responsive to customer needs.

## A FOCUS ON QUALITY

The other part of the training that I think is unique is that we actually require new people to focus on quality, not productivity. We observe 100 percent of their cases during the learning period, and not until they get their quality up to 100 percent do we worry about whether they are meeting their productivity goals.

To help us measure the quality of calls, we did an attribute study with customers on what we call "treatment" and "resolution." Treatment is the emotional, affective side of the call; resolution refers to process, accuracy, and compliance. Customer focus groups determine the key drivers of satisfaction (for example, politeness and knowledge) for both treatment and resolution, and we train the representatives to deliver those attributes. We have also used Ph.Ds and behavioral psychologists to help us effectively train team leaders and supervisors to be experts in active listening.

In addition, supervisors, team leaders, and directors go out onto the floor every month and monitor the telephone calls. They then give the telephone representatives feedback as to how well they are doing in terms of both behavioral characteristics and tactical responses. It is a very extensive monitoring, coaching, feedback, and surveying process.

## LEARNING TO LISTEN

One of the things we do as part of our training class is to teach our employees how to be active listeners. We want them to hear what a customer is saying, repeat it back to the customer, and then set expectations about what the conclusion of the call is going to be. Unless people can actively listen, they can't learn from the customer. Once they possess the skill of active listening, they can basically learn what customers' needs are and communicate those needs to the organization in order to solve problems or invent new products.

In fact, we have made a huge investment in customer listening and customer measurement. We use key transactions, such as card replacement and new program enrollments, as opportunities to survey our customers to make sure that we are meeting their expectations for timeliness and accuracy. We also gather customer focus group research to supplement survey information.

In addition to enhancing our customer service, we use customer listening to make improvements in the product line. As part of our small business program, for example, American Express regularly brings together a panel of small business owners to make sure we are meeting the special needs of this group. As a result, we have developed programs that provide American Express Small Business customers with secure equipment financing and special rates for package delivery, travel, and gasoline.

In addition, Small Business cards provide a level of detail and documentation with the monthly statement that helps small firms manage their expenses. Also, we provide special quarterly management reports that summarize spending by category and employee.

Rather than taking a standard approach to treating every customer exactly the same way, American Express encourages its employees to assess each individual situation, listen to the nuances, and then go beyond the obvious. Skills and techniques are combined with positive employee attitudes to deliver superior customer service.

## A Cultural Orientation

Most significant is the cultural orientation that it takes to achieve this degree of personal service. We track employee dedication to customer service in our yearly employee surveys. In fact, our employees and our technology give us a real competitive advantage that is difficult for other credit-card companies to copy.

A good example of the mind-set that accompanies a buy-in of that magnitude occurred recently when representatives asked to hear what they sound like when talking to customers. Some employees had received feedback during their coaching sessions that recommended a greater sense of flexibility and a more positive tone of voice. Since it is difficult for some of us to hear the way we sound in a conversation, we implemented a call-recording function. With a customer's permission, a call can be recorded and then played back as the supervisor and the customer service representative listen in together and decide together how to improve customer service.

## THE ONE-TO-ONE CONNECTION

Database technology is expanding the possibilities for initiating conversations with individual customers. For example, we focus on individual customer needs when we receive calls from customers related to service or maintenance issues. By using our vast database, we can recommend products or services they don't already have that would seem to be relevant to their lifestyle.

Let's say that a certain customer who travels twelve times a month doesn't have baggage insurance. The likely correlation is that this product would be of interest to her, and she just might not know that we offer this service at a competitive price. So if that customer calls us with a question about her billing sheet or spending limit, we can offer her baggage insurance in the course of handling the query, right on the spot.

One of the exciting things about customer-focused selling is that we have increased both customer satisfaction and employee satisfaction. This channel is a great way to have meaningful conversations with customers and provide them with additional value at their convenience—and be driven by their desire to contact us. Because we've managed to do this in a consultative environment, customers actually feel that we're discovering additional value with them.

## MERCHANTS ARE CUSTOMERS, TOO

We know that the merchant plays a key part in how cardholders feel about American Express, which is why we consider them both our customers. With our CustomExtras program both these groups receive value out of a transaction. We bring a valuable offer to the cardmember and help the merchant target new and loyal customers.

Express Rewards is another one-to-one marketing program that gives merchants a way to build customer loyalty. The program provides valued customers with special rewards at the point of purchase. The program works in real time; at a predetermined point, a customer who makes repeat purchases at a particular place of business will trigger a VIP signal that alerts the merchant to reward this loyal customer.

Here's a case in point. Let's say there is a customer who eats at a particular restaurant on a regular basis, each time paying with his American Express Card. After a certain number of visits by this patron, the cashier at this participating restaurant will see the "VIP Customer" symbol appear when clearing the customer's card. This will indicate to the cashier that the customer is eligible for a predetermined award: "We appreciate your regular patronage. To thank you for dining with us tonight, your bottle of wine is on the house!"

It's a great way to make people feel special without their expecting it. And it gives merchants a worldwide reward-and-recognition system that they don't have to duplicate themselves. We supply all the infrastructure for them.

## COMING TO THE RESCUE

One of the most common and innovative forms of one-to-one customer contact occurs when a customer service representative aids a traveler in trouble. Even if you're stranded in a remote place, you can often find an American Express office: We're in 160 countries around the world. But if you need to call one of our U.S. centers and contact us directly, you can do so by calling collect to the number listed on the back of your card.

Derrick, a customer service representative in Utah and another of our "Great Performers" for 1996, played guardian angel to an Australian cardmember who inadvertently left his cash, traveler's checks, and other valuables in a safe-deposit box at a hotel in Anaheim, California. Being without funds is problem enough, but further complicating matters was the fact that the cardmember didn't realize his predicament until he arrived in England to continue his holiday.

When Derrick got the call, he first contacted the hotel to have the needed property turned over to American Express for delivery to the cardmember in England. The hotel wouldn't do so until it had a notarized request from the owner, so Derrick called the cardmember and secured a notarized letter. Letter in hand, Derrick called the American Express Travel Office in Anaheim, where two employees were dispatched to the hotel to pick up the cardmember's belongings.

While the California employees shipped the items via overnight mail to England, Derrick contacted the cardmember yet again to tell him his belongings were on their way. Because Derrick didn't hesitate to go out of his way for a single customer, the Australian vacationer was able to enjoy the rest of his trip with hardly a ripple of inconvenience.

## PROTECTING CUSTOMERS' PRIVACY

Sometimes having a reputation as a premier service provider is just the impetus naysayers need. Someone always likes to recount a horror story or two that takes some of the shine off a top-notch player. And with 41.5 million customers, American Express occasionally encounters dissatisfaction.

In general, we have a very extensive process in place to handle mistakes, real or perceived. And we go to great lengths to uncover and address any complaints, but to pro-

tect customer privacy, we will not disclose specific inci-
dences. Customer problems coming in to representatives at
the floor level can travel up the chain of command until
someone in a senior position winds up resolving the problem. We have an executive correspondence process that,
with the help of our legal department, reviews and responds
to calls and letters made to the chairman, the president, or
one of the division presidents.

Unlike other powerful, well-known, worldwide brands,
however, American Express is not always free to stage a
public counterattack when unfair or untrue publicity surfaces. There are times when a customer may say things we
choose not to refute, because to do so would require our
divulging customer information to the press. We don't do
that. If someone contends, for example, that a can of soda
didn't taste right or that a can or bottle contained a foreign
object, the manufacturer of that soda can respond to the
charges. But even if we can prove the customer wrong, we
don't divulge information because we value the customer's
right to confidentiality.

## MEETING TOMORROW'S CHALLENGES

In terms of our worldwide aspirations, the next three to
five years will present a huge opportunity to further glob-
alize our business and fulfill our corporate vision of
becoming the world's most respected service brand. I
believe there is an unparalleled opening here for us to provide service on a global basis, even though cultures and

expectations vary tremendously worldwide. The key is the basic functionality that we are now building, which ties that robust database to econometric models to expert systems—the same package that will soon help guide a representative through various customer transactions. Taking into account that different countries have varying viewpoints on customer service, the package will be able to address these differences.

When that package is put in front of representatives worldwide, customers everywhere will be treated as they expect to be treated, based on their history and their input. Such an environment will allow customer service representatives to accommodate local differences while establishing a global brand. I think that portends tremendous power.

As for changes within the industry, particularly the growing usage of bank debit cards, our strategy revolves around aggressively making our service capabilities and our merchant network available to other business partners on a global basis. As our chairman announced in the spring of 1997, we are "opening our network." Business partners who want to issue our cards with us or use our network to access our merchants are now able to do that in more than twenty-five countries around the world.

We want to extend our brand and our merchant network to enhance the value they bring to a broad group of customers. We have the ability to make partnerships work globally and are expanding them very rapidly. This puts us well on the way to becoming the world's most respected service brand.

■■■

## AMERICAN EXPRESS COMPANY

## COMPANY PROFILE

| | |
|---|---|
| Business Description | Financial, travel, and network services |
| Website | www.americanexpress.com |
| Founded | 1850 |
| Annual Sales | $17.7 billion |
| Net Income | $1.99 billion |
| Employees | 72,300 |
| Products | American Express cards |
| | American Express Traveler's Cheques |
| | Banking services |
| | Corporate Card |
| | Financial planning services |
| | Property/casualty insurance |
| | Revolving credit cards (Optima) |
| | Travel planning |
| Magazines | *Departures* |
| | *Food & Wine* |
| | *Travel & Leisure* |
| | *Your Company* |

*The keys to customer service today are keeping customers for life, fostering loyalty, and cementing relationships. Noble thoughts all, but have you ever considered how few products the typical customer sticks with over an extended period? Here's a simple exercise: Try to put together a list of brands or products that you have been buying for more than, say, ten or fifteen years. I bet your list won't be long—and that some of the names will surprise you. Clearly, keeping customers glued to your product for an extended period isn't as easy as it may sound.*

*While reflecting on this, it dawned on me that I've been a American Express "member" for almost twenty-five years. Twenty-five years! That's longer than I've known my wife. That's longer than I've lived in any city, and longer than I've used any one brand. Come to think of it, it's longer than I've done business with any other company. It's not that I've been constantly enamored with American Express. There have been occasions where the organization outright irritated me. I've had my share of customer service run-ins with its representatives. And, to tell the truth, I've told more than a few unflattering stories about the company.*

*So what makes me, together with millions of others, a loyal customer? Why do I without hesitation pay an annual $75 fee for the "privilege" of membership when other highly reputable firms constantly entice me with offers of free cards? Why do I willingly pay another $25 to take part in this company's frequent-user program (Membership Rewards) when all the similar programs I belong to don't cost me anything? Why do I instinctively pull my American Express card from my wallet, leaving other cards largely untouched?*

*The answer lies only partly in the brand's aura and the habits I've formed. My perceptions and priorities have changed. My buying patterns have evolved. My expectations have risen, and my choices have become better than ever. So the best explanation I have for my ongoing use of* the card is that American Express is constantly evolving its offerings in its quest for share-of-wallet. Call it service innovation. Call it keeping abreast of customer needs. Call it a marketing classic.

At American Express you'll notice less of the warm-and-fuzzies, the folksiness that typifies some of the other companies in this book. American Express cuts a different impression: more reserved, less inclined to show a rah-rah attitude; more analytically oriented. Unsurprisingly, the company relies on information technology as a source of customer knowledge and service innovation—perhaps more so than other organizations in this book. The notion of building and tracking profiles on every person it interacts with is very important. If Customer A differs from Customer B, American Express wants to understand how. Almost from the moment the phone rings into the customer service desk, representatives know who's on the line—and what their background and history with the company has been. American Express looks for any way it can to improve efficiency while at the same time keeping its customer profiles up-to-date. I wouldn't be surprised if in many ways this company knew more about what makes customers tick than those customers know themselves.

Based on the American Express example, several thoughts come to mind for building stronger bonds with customers:

- Think customer longevity. Get everyone tuned in to its importance. You may be surprised to discover how little you know about which customers have been with you the longest—and why. Remedy that ignorance by contacting them to uncover what keeps them so loyal. At the same time, explore what might have triggered other customers to leave you.

- Figure out what you can do to stop these defections. Is there a way to recapture and reengage lost customers? (American Express cards have the inscription "Member since 19xx." Doesn't that say a lot about the company's longtime orientation toward keeping customers?)

- Be on the alert for changing customer habits. Keep a finger on the pulse—try to discern changing patterns of behavior, as well as changing attitudes and expectations. Are you noticing any trends? Are you keeping up with all of them? Is your customer service staff briefed on what's happening in the marketplace? Remember, change can be your friend—but only if you're better at dealing with it than your rivals.

- Upgrade your consumer intelligence. Get serious about building a richer customer database. Make sure you capture each customer's buying and service history. There's plenty of software available today to get better informed while enhancing your customer service responsiveness and accuracy. Take advantage of it.

- Reward customer loyalty. Create your own frequent-user program. Find ways to recognize and appreciate repeat purchasers and longtime customers, even if they aren't the biggest spenders. Get your customer service operations to reflect that there's no better customer than a loyal one. And always remind your customers that you're on their side.

# 5

## Staples, Inc.

*Offer the Personal Touch*

*T*hat Staples, Inc. (www.staples.com) excels in the area of customer satisfaction should come as no surprise. After all, the idea behind the founding of the company in 1986 was to provide a particular consumer segment— small-business owners—with the same heavily discounted prices on office supplies that large corporations enjoyed.

By the mid-1980s, low cost and variety were already a long-established combination available to people shopping for groceries and clothing. It was, in fact, former super-market executive Thomas Stemberg who believed the changing American business landscape suggested that the same modern mass-distribution techniques used in those industries could be applied to the office-supply market. He saw that of 11 million companies operating in the United States in 1985, 10.8 million were classified as small businesses. Most of these were run by hands-on owners who purchased their own supplies. Add to this the growing *number of two-income families with personal computers, and the result was a record number of home offices popping up, all or most in need of furniture, software, copiers, and other business necessities.*

*Stemberg's hunch was right-on. A lone wolf when it first opened its doors in Brighton, Massachusetts, on May 1, 1986, Staples, Inc., grew to include twenty stores within two years—and attracted twenty competitors. Between 1989 and 1995, Staples opened a new branch every eight days, and by the end of 1997 the company surpassed $5 billion in annual sales—only the seventh company in U.S. business history to reach that level within twelve years. By April 1998, there were more than seven hundred Staples stores in North America, as well as fifty-eight more in Germany and the United Kingdom.*

*Offering more than 7,600 brand-name office products, office furniture, business machines, computers, software, FedEx ship sites, and full-service copy centers, all at every-day low prices, Staples is living up to its self-billing as "The Office Superstore." But in a now mature industry that includes staunch competitors such as Office Max and Office Depot, it has become harder and harder to distinguish one chain from another: They all sell Post-it notes and paper clips at low prices. In order to stand out, Staples is building an increasingly innovative customer service program, providing added value, cultivating personal relationships with its customers, and continuously improving the way it does business.*

*If they can't sell a product for less than their competi-*

*tors, Stemberg and his staff still want to give each customer the best deal possible—and the best buying experience.*

## JIM PETERS
### President, U.S. Stores

Although Staples has grown to be a $5 billion-plus company, we work hard to give it the flavor of a small store with an entrepreneurial spirit. When we train managers and sales associates, for instance, our orientation program emphasizes the history of the company—how and why it got started, why we're successful, and how we're a benefit to the customer.

For hourly employees, we have what we call a scavenger-hunt test. First, the new hires are taken around the store with a buddy to learn about stocking. Then they are given a list of a hundred items and told to find where each is located. We don't time them—it's not important that they do it in fifteen minutes. We just want them to understand exactly where products go. If a customer comes in and asks where the ballpoint pens are, you can't just say, "aisle 3"—because a customer will go there and find 350 different pens. We want our associates to take a customer to the aisle, put the pen in his hand, and then wait to make sure he is satisfied that this is the pen he wants.

## RALLYING AROUND THE MESSAGE

For about ten minutes twice a day, we have what we call rally meetings in every one of our stores. The general manager calls the staff together each morning before the store opens—then again late in the afternoon, when the second shift comes on—to talk about how things went the previous day. And rather than just discuss sales in these meetings, the manager almost always focuses on customer service. For instance, the manager might say, "Yesterday a customer wanted to return a package of diskettes and some software but didn't have a receipt. We didn't handle that request well, and this is what we should have done." The goal is to teach and train the whole group rather than single out and criticize one associate.

These meetings offer opportunities for some very creative learning. Sometimes, a manager will hand an associate $10 or $20, with instructions to visit a competitor or another retail store and make a purchase. The employee makes the trip during his or her shift, then reports back to the group at the next day's meeting with an analysis of the competitor's customer service capabilities.

Next, the manager might say, "Okay, now return the product—without the receipt." This leads to a whole new set of questions the associate will have to field the next day: "Were you hassled? Did the competitor's employees give you a hard time? Did they actually take the return?" Again, it's one thing for me as a manager to stand up there every day and talk about how we want to treat our customers. But it's another thing for an associate to come back and say, "You know, I had to stand in line a long time," or "I was looking for the product. Everybody could see I was looking for it, but none of the employees approached me to ask if I needed help."

We work hard to teach our people that great service is critical, and we empower our associates to take care of the customer at practically any cost. Our typical customer shops in our store once every eighteen days and spends $40 during each visit. We spend millions of dollars a year to get customers into our stores. Once we get them there, we can't afford to lose them.

## STRIVING FOR CONTINUOUS IMPROVEMENT

Staples is an entrepreneurial company, and its culture is intense. An idea can come from anybody at any level—a stocker in a store or a director at the executive office. Anyone can come up with a concept to make us operate more efficiently or give us an edge in customer service. And although we have a strong operational structure, we are flexible enough to allow people to try something new if they think it's going to lead to more efficient, improved service down the line.

One group of employees, for example, came up with the idea for our "Concept 97" store, a technology center inside a regular Staples branch where we can upgrade personal computers, install a new port, or check for general computer problems. This new concept is being rolled out in all stores during 1998. For contributing their ideas, we reward employees with shares of Staples stock—not cash—because we want people to become owners of their company.

## NO SURPRISES

Most customers want to find the right product in the right place at the right time and in the right package—with no surprises. Look at what such great retailers as McDonald's and the Ritz-Carlton Hotels do. Buy a McDonald's hamburger in New York or Tokyo, and in either city you can be sure of getting the same product: the same bun, patty, onion, two pickles, ketchup, and mustard. It's the same with Ritz-Carlton. Whether you're in San Francisco or London, your wake-up call is exactly the same: "Good morning, Mr. Peters, it's twenty-two degrees outside." Great retail chains understand how important it is to provide a consistent set of nuts and bolts for each product or experience.

This consistency is crucial. I'm not saying we want our managers to be robots who don't think for themselves; we just don't want them to have to think about pieces of the daily operations that *should* be consistent. They should not worry, for instance, about how products are coming into the store. They should, however, be concerned with more significant questions: "How do I develop my staff? How do I connect with the community? How do I engage in a closer relationship with my customers?" Only by taking away the obstacles can you encourage a more entrepreneurial spirit as well as a more creative approach. Our managers should be focused on only three things—the customer, the associate, and the community. That's how we can build our business.

Our customers are often on a first-name basis with the managers and many of the associates in our stores. This is a great way to build a sense of community. If the same person is coming into a Staples store every eighteen days, and we get to know her and treat her with a sense of professionalism and respect, she's not going to leave us for one of our competitors. She knows the product she's looking for is always going to be on the shelf and the price is always going to be fair. And if all those things are true, and if she also knows the people there are going to be friendly and helpful, why would she ever want to go somewhere else?

## LOOK, LISTEN, AND LEARN

We track a lot of information about our customers, and through a direct mailing or similar promotional offer, we can target those who have stopped shopping with us. To evaluate how we're being perceived in the marketplace, we conduct focus groups throughout the year. If associates at one of our stores notice that customers are requesting a product that is constantly out of stock, the associates can use a form to notify our merchandising group to increase or change an order. In addition to the items we regularly carry, our stores have access to twenty-five thousand more items through a special-order catalog. Each store tracks orders from the catalog, and if something is constantly being special-ordered, the lightbulb should go off in someone's head and that store should begin to carry that product.

The name of the game is meeting customer expectations. In focus group after focus group, the majority of our customers tell us that we don't have to exceed their expectations—just meet them. They want to come to the store, find what they need, buy the quantity they want, and leave expeditiously. They want to shop in a clean store, with knowledgeable, friendly associates, where they can find what they need at the right price. They don't wake up in the morning thinking, "I'm going to go buy some legal pads and Post-it notes today! I can't wait!" They come in because they have to come in. Our job is to make sure their shopping experience absolutely meets their expectations.

Not all our customers share this expectation, of course. Some want to be taken around the store, be shown various options, and be told how products work. Perhaps a boss has asked a worker to pick up some third-cut file folders, but the worker doesn't have the foggiest idea what a third-cut folder is or how it differs from a fifth-cut folder. In this situation, a Staples associate will spend a few minutes showing this customer the difference, as well as help with all the other items on the worker's shopping list.

## STUDY THE BEST

At Staples, we would prefer to be known not as the best retailer in the world but as the best service business around. To earn that reputation, we benchmark against other retailers, not necessarily those in the office-supply industry. That's why we look at organizations such as McDonald's and Ritz-Carlton, premier companies that are decidedly service-oriented.

There's a hamburger chain on the West Coast called In-N-Out Burger. These restaurants employ the friendliest people in the fast-food business, bar none. Every time I eat in one, I say, "How come they're doing such a great job?"

They're flipping burgers—most people hate flipping burgers. But visit one of their stores, and you'll see how truly amazing they are and how seriously they take the job of helping customers.

To build a service culture like that, you must recruit well. It's not enough to run an ad or put up a "Help Wanted" sign on your door. What you need to find in workers is attitude as much as skills. You can teach anybody to ring a cash register, but you can't teach everybody to be friendly and outgoing. If you start with that quality, the rest is easy. If you don't have that to start with, you lose.

*All customer service calls and letters sent to Staples—between 1,200 and 1,400 of them each month from throughout the United States—come into the department of customer service development at the company's Westborough, Massachusetts, headquarters. Headed by Lynne Broderick, this department does far more than answer phones and letters. It handles every customer service initiative undertaken by the company. This includes the mystery-shopper program—a means of measuring how well Staples responds to customer needs at the point of contact in each store—as well as the development of training programs.*

## LYNNE BRODERICK
### Manager of Customer Service Development

Only five representatives handle all the calls and letters that come into our department, yet we don't allow ourselves to be driven by such numbers as the amount of time needed to handle a call. Part of the process of satisfying disgruntled customers is letting them vent—which can take anywhere from two to ten minutes. You have to be willing to be patient.

Ideally, the general manager at the store in which a problem occurs should handle the dissatisfied customer. Not only is it aggravating to the customer and costly for us to take the call, but most customers don't want to have to deal with making multiple phone calls concerning the same issue. So in the best scenario, the problem is taken care of in the store. We don't want customers ever to leave the store with a dilemma unresolved.

The general manager of the store in which the incident occurred is notified so that he or she can discuss the problem with the associate who dealt with the unhappy customer. In most cases, the manager calls the customer, offers an apology, and explains what Staples is doing to rectify the situation. A customer relations representative also calls most customers who have made complaints to make sure everything is cleared up. If the issue is more serious, we bring in district managers and directors of operations to address the issue with the store and contact the customer.

The store associate involved rarely calls the customer because we don't think it's wise to have two people who didn't have a good common experience talk again. (The exception occurs when customers want a verbal apology from the person who dealt with them.) This practice also lets the customer know that we've elevated this complaint to the managerial level. The customer may not always be right, but Staples still recognizes the value of each customer to the company. And if that customer has a perception—right or wrong—of discourteous or unfair behavior or actions, that's something real to us and worth investigating.

Our most common complaints revolve around courtesy, which can be broadly interpreted. "Courtesy" can include the sales associate's knowledge of products, along with how helpful and available he or she is to the customer. We find that customers sometimes misinterpret a behavior as rude or discourteous because there is poor communication or poor understanding of process or policy. For the sake of customer satisfaction, we often break our own rules.

We have a thirty-day return policy on all our products, with the exception of computers and printers—which carry a fourteen-day return policy. This is, however, an area in which we can be flexible. A customer could have a stapler for four years, then decide he or she doesn't like the way it's working anymore and try to return it. We would probably take that stapler back or give the customer a coupon for the original purchase price. The exchange is small, but what we gain in customer service is huge. That customer isn't going to forget the gesture.

## TECHNOLOGY TO THE RESCUE
In 1996, we installed a great database and network at headquarters to support our customer service program. Once we register a complaint into this system, we fax it right out to

the general manager of the store in which the incident occurred. Depending on the severity of the episode, we also send it to various high-ranking managers. Our database is a Lotus Notes software program that we developed ourselves and then had tweaked by experts to work on customer service issues. Our system can track duplications, so we know who those customers are who contact us repeatedly. We never close a case unless we receive confirmation from a manager that a follow-up between the manager, customer, and associate has taken place. Often, we also call the customers to make sure they are satisfied.

## THE C.A.R.E. PROGRAM

We introduced a companywide effort in 1995 aimed at getting our employees to provide stellar customer service every day. The C.A.R.E. Program serves as the foundation for everything we do here. It's built around our four most important priorities: our Customers, our Associates, the Real communications that keep us connected to both groups, and the job Execution of our managers and associates at all levels. As part of this program, we have each store employee go through hour-long training sessions that comprise the following modules:

- **Staples Customer Service Strategy:** This module introduces our C.A.R.E. values and describes in detail what each letter stands for. It's the basis for the way we currently do business, as well as a look at how we might improve the way we do business in the future.

- **Staples Customer Service Standards:** In this module, we describe exactly what our standards are. We review the comment-card program and how we use it to improve our customer service performance. We also teach when and how to provide proactive customer service.
- **The ABCs of Juggling Customers and Jobs:** The premise and target of this module came directly from customer feedback. The module shows various tricks of the trade, such as how to achieve great service while assisting two or more customers at the same time or while also engaged in other tasks.
- **The Seven Keys to Managing Customer Expectations:** This module gets to the heart of what our customers tell us they want from us. It addresses the seven primary customer expectations for Staples, which are derived from focus groups, comment cards, and the underperforming areas uncovered by mystery shoppers. [These three areas are discussed in detail later in the chapter.]
- **Managing Irate or Difficult Customers:** This module, which is still in development, will instruct employees whose job it is to manage customers who are difficult to handle, extremely unhappy, angry, or all three. It will be geared mostly toward managers, customer service representatives, and technical center associates—the people most likely to deal with these customers.

159

We are now in the process of moving these modules into a dual format so that we can do multimedia workshops with a group of employees or individualized training with one employee in front of a PC. One of these computers will be available in every store, and our people will have options in choosing the modules.

It's up to the management team in each store to make sure their associates receive the training they need. If they don't pass the certification tests at the end of each module, the associates must repeat the module. The tests are not intended to force workers to memorize intricate formulas and procedures but rather to test basic understanding.

## MYSTERY SHOPPING

To measure compliance with established standards—as well as to gauge the effectiveness of the C.A.R.E. program—we established our mystery-shopping program four years ago. We contract with an external company, which each month sends a mystery shopper portraying an average customer into every one of our stores. Because we go to great lengths to make sure we don't get repeat mystery shoppers going into the same stores, the visits always go undetected. The goal of the visits is to measure each store's compliance with the standards we have in place, as well as to focus on the selling skills of the store employees. We measure six basic categories of standards:

- **General Standards:** We look at uniform conformance—whether the store is neat and clean, the employees are well groomed, the associates are friendly and attentive, as well as other parameters.

- **Special-Order Standards:** Many people don't know we have a program through which customers can take advantage of twenty-five thousand items beyond those we regularly carry in the store, by ordering through the special-order catalog. So when the mystery shoppers ask employees for something we don't carry, they are checking whether the employees go to the special-order catalog to help customers through the ordering process.

- **Checkout Standards:** Mystery shoppers study what the checkout process is like for customers from the moment they step into the register line. We evaluate wait time, friendliness of checkout personnel, and accuracy.

- **Return Standards:** Each mystery shopper goes through the process of returning an item to make sure this is a hassle-free process.

- **Copy Center Standards:** The mystery shopper also goes through the process of having a copy order produced, checking on everything from greet time to order quality to the reasons why an order may not have been completed when promised.

- **Business Machine Sales Standards:** This is probably the most important aspect of mystery shopping. Here we're evaluating the sales associate's knowledge of products and selling skills in the business machine area. Because these are the most expensive items we carry, we need these salespeople to know exactly what they're selling.

The whole program speaks loudly to basic customer service: Greet customers in a friendly, courteous manner, assist them as needed, and help them get out of the store quickly. The standards we measure against change each year, based on customer feedback. But the general thinking behind mystery shopping remains tied to those six basic elements.

Because all stores are evaluated each month and any changes we make are across the board, we devised a scoring system that measures improvement over time. Each store is measured on a hundred-point scale, with questions weighted differently. So a "yes" answer gets you a varying number of points based on how important that area is to overall store performance.

Once the mystery shoppers fill out their forms, they call in the scores to the mystery-shopping vendor. Quality control then verifies the accuracy of the score and the shopping process, after which everything is entered into a computer system and tallied. The final scores are faxed to the general manager of each store.

In each mystery-shopping category, we get a name or description of the person the shopper interacted with. Because the tally is done so quickly, the results can be used to coach store employees. Each store general manager can post the monthly scores in the employees' break room, where we have set up a mystery-shopper board so that the staff can see the results and gauge improvement.

The process doesn't end with our faxing the scores to the individual stores. District managers work closely with each general manager to make sure they work on problem areas. It works the same way all the down the chain: Regional people work with district managers, and the national office oversees the whole process. We track categories and questions and analyze which stores are performing noticeably well or poorly.

But we don't measure stores solely on mystery-shopping performance. Each Staples store also prominently displays comment cards that customers can fill out and send in. We receive about five thousand of these cards each month from across the country, and they are an excellent means of assessing how people view the stores. Then, of course, there are the customer complaints and compliments that come to us in the form of letters, phone calls, and Website responses. We get approximately sixteen thousand customer contacts annually through these media, which we track back to the store in which each incident took place.

From all this input, we have developed a customer service index—or CSI—made up of three measures for store performance: mystery shopping, comment cards, and other customer feedback. We calculate a score in each area for each store, and we reward the stores that score in the top twentieth percentile each quarter. This is a team-based award, so we give each winning staff money that is to be used for a group effort—a holiday party, a cookout, a donation to charity, or whatever else they want. Each year, after we look at the different kinds of compensation programs that might best motivate the people who work in our stores, we wind up sticking with this: Our associates seem to love being able to do what they want with the money.

## THE COST OF CUSTOMER SERVICE

You can't fool customers by simply waving a flag that says "customer service." And you can't fool them into thinking you're making significant improvements in customer service if you're not doing so. You need to back up your promises, financially and with actions, before customers begin to see a difference.

If you can get the store manager and maybe two or three people in each store really focused on setting an example, talking about customer service every day, and regularly giving other employees coaching and feedback, I think you've found the driver. Not everybody is cut out to be a customer service provider. You have to hire the right people. We're very clear as a company about what our expectations are, and we help people develop plans to get there.

### JACKIE SHOBACK
#### Vice President, Staples Call Center Operations

Our call centers offer items from our regular quarterly Staples catalog and from our annual special-order catalog. The regular catalog lists 4,000 to 5,000 of the 7,600 items we offer in our stores; the special-order catalog gives customers access to as many as 25,000 additional products. These special orders are fulfilled and delivered through third-party vendors. We advertise next-day delivery on the cover of our regular catalog. For special orders, it usually takes us from three to five business days to deliver an order to a customer.

As you might expect, customer service issues arise from using these vendors and from our consequent ability to give our customers the level of satisfaction they demand. Some of our customers, for instance, want a unique custom stamp or a ribbon for an old typewriter. Our special-order catalog usually has what the customer needs. More than likely, if you can't find something in a Staples store or in our regular catalog, we'll be able to get it for you through this alternate source. So from a service standpoint, our specialty-items offering has allowed us to get hard-to-find products for customers when they need them.

Both the regular and the special-order catalogs are mailed to customers. The quarterly catalogs go to all customers; the annual catalog is typically reserved for groups we think might want it based on the purchasing behaviors they have shown in the past. There is always room for error, of course, and customers can always call in and request a special-order catalog.

## TRAINING FOR SUCCESS

All our associates go through a rigorous training program. We start off with two weeks of classroom training that prepare our new hires to take a typical sales call. These simple and straightforward calls comprise the majority of calls we handle. Customers making such calls—which we consider our bread and butter—usually have a catalog from which they have selected items and would like to place an order. After taking these calls for a while, associates move into the position of "universal" representative—that is, someone who can handle any call on any issue that comes in.

We find this development process beneficial from a couple of standpoints. Customers like the fact that they can reach a person who will take a new order, as well as process changes to existing orders, with the same level of ease and without transferring the call. We try to give our customers a single point of contact so that the order entry and servicing process is as easy as possible from a customer's perspective. With universal representatives, customer service becomes everyone's job; it is not reserved for one group that just handles problems.

The average associate trains for about six months, including on-the-floor sales experience and time spent gaining familiarity with our product lines. With the many additional items in our special-order catalog, a call center associate can often find a substitute for an out-of-stock product, a service that can prove very helpful to the customer. Sales experience also teaches people patience and empathy, two valuable traits in delivering customer service. Because many customers call us before knowing precisely what they want, they appreciate an associate who takes time to listen to their needs and offers recommendations.

The words I most frequently hear to describe our representatives are patient, helpful, pleasant.

The philosophy that guides our work is: Let the people closest to the work make things work better. This operating philosophy helps us take care of the customer. For instance, our associates have given us new ideas and have challenged existing policies they believed were hampering customer service.

We used to be more strict about our price guarantees, requiring a customer to fax in the competitor's advertisement with the lower price before we would complete a price match. But we found that more often than not, customers calling in for a price guarantee were referencing an advertisement the Staples associate had already seen.

Accordingly, we empowered our associates to use their judgment in executing the price match. If they were already aware of the competitor's advertised price, for instance, they could simplify the process by telling a customer he or she didn't have to bother faxing in the competitor's ad. We simply didn't want our customers or our associates to go through all those hoops if they already had the information they needed to make an informed decision.

## GETTING THE FUNDAMENTALS UNDER CONTROL

Customer service at many companies seems to be a defensive mechanism, an attempt to cover up mistakes that never should have occurred in the first place. We don't want this to happen at Staples. We use our computer system to log in every customer call and complaint and make this information available to our associates. We want them to know exactly what's going on.

Capturing this information also allows us to do additional reporting and analysis. For instance, we track every service issue we encounter—returns, missing items, credits, exchanges—and as soon as a peculiar trend surfaces, we flag it. For example, we were having sporadic problems with our outbound faxing equipment. The equipment wasn't always working properly, and by surfacing the main issues, we were able to pinpoint what was going wrong and make the proper changes.

Providing great customer service is a difficult job, no question about it. There are lots of details to master, and it takes more than putting together the right people and instilling customer service as a value in the corporate culture.

I'll give you an example. Here in the call center, we have a monthly meeting at which people on my staff get together with people from distribution. We call it the "service improvement meeting." We talk about our customer satisfaction numbers and any operational problems we're encountering. Where do we need to improve? What are the issues on the rise? Do our customers report damages in shipments? Do incomplete orders arrive?

We conduct trend analyses to see whether we're getting better or worse. In fact, we have an elaborate coding system with which we identify problems and issues and then key them to each order. You might say we are a bit obsessed with tracking and analyzing, but we're doing it so that we can always improve. Ultimately we can ask ourselves, "What's going on with this customer? Do we need to do something? Is this problem indicative of a bigger issue at Staples? Do we need to change something?"

It may surprise you to learn that we call all our top customers once a year. That is unique to our culture and approach at Staples. We call to thank the customers for their business and to ask them which areas of the company they think we can improve. And it's not just the call center folks who make these calls; all of Staples Direct management participates in the undertaking. Our customers are usually impressed with this display of effort and often offer suggestions that we then evaluate for implementation.

One suggestion we've acted on in the call centers is the request by our top customers to reduce their information verification during order entry. Our associates know that if a top customer is placing an order, they don't need to verify all the customer's information—much of it has not changed since the last order. We are always trying to make our process as simple as possible for the customer.

## Recognizing Employees

Direct Effect is a call center employee-recognition program through which our associates nominate someone from within the call centers who they think is providing excellent customer service. Each quarter, the call centers have a ceremony during which we read off all the nominees' accomplishments, then give an engraved pen to each of them, along with a $50 cash award. It's a big celebration, and everyone is invited. Winners are not chosen by management but by the Direct Effect board of associates who evaluate the anonymous nominations.

Employees who win twice within four quarters are designated Direct Effect Gold winners. As part of their reward, they travel to a Staples facility of their choice in the United States and spend one day shadowing its manager. Or, if they prefer, they can go to a seminar to enhance their development. The idea is to broaden their horizons, enabling them to see other opportunities in the company.

In addition, our quarterly Tommy Award is a special corporatewide recognition that singles out any individual or group that comes up with an idea that is innovative and makes a significant impact on the company's financial success. One of our Direct Effect winners, Skip, was given a Tommy for his Extra Call Program. Having worked in the credit industry before joining the Staples staff, Skip recognized that many companies could be turned down for credit simply because they did not have sufficient time to build a solid credit history.

"I knew that if I called back on a lot of these accounts, I could overturn the credit rejection," says Skip. "I bet I could turn rejections into approvals just by asking the credit provider to look at some other parameters."

Skip was sure that making this request would help his case. So he established a group of contacts at our credit provider—a third party—and made an "extra call" on those companies he believed were good candidates for credit approvals. In the end, he was able to generate significant incremental sales just by calling back the credit provider and asking, "Did you check these other areas?"

Skip's success illustrates one of the things I appreciate most about working at Staples. I've always enjoyed the sense of ownership that pervades this place, a sense that if you have a passion and you want to take action or make a difference, you can. It's not about having a great idea and passing it off to someone else. It's having a great idea and thinking through how to make it happen, then coming up with the way to do it. Since I've been here, Staples has always been willing to take a chance and try something different.

When I was working in one of our city-based stores, we had a group of customers who didn't like calling our toll-free delivery number because they wanted to pick out items in person. At the same time, however, they sometimes wanted their boxes carried for them a couple of blocks. My associates would not hesitate to help them. We also knew our store was a little small because it was in the city. So if there was something special these customers wanted that we didn't have, we would call around to another store and find it for them. Then, on my way home, I'd stop by the other store, pick up the item, and bring it to the customer's home.

I'm sure our top customers are surprised to get a call from us thanking them for their business and asking them to tell us how we can improve. But soliciting ideas from a customer and then finding ways to implement them is a valuable process for us. Many associates who have been here a long time have learned to understand what the customer is looking for, and this has become a tremendously useful resource.

*As the Staples Direct unit of Staples and the retail stores were gaining momentum within the small-business market, it became clear there was another important segment of the market that Staples could serve—medium- to large-size businesses. These larger businesses typically purchase office supplies via negotiated contracts based on their purchasing volume and frequency. Staples introduced two new operations: Staples Business Advantage, which caters to regional medium- to large-size companies, and Staples National Advantage, which serves national Fortune 1000, multisite companies. Although the contract customer is different from the store and the catalog shopper, customer service remains a critical component of the division's and the company's success.*

### EVAN STERN
#### President, Staples National Advantage

Field sales representatives are not providers of customer service. They deal primarily with purchasers who, in turn, are not really customers. In the true sense of the word, the customer is the person that requisitions the goods—the one at the end of the line.

I think that most companies fool themselves into thinking that the director of purchasing is the customer. But this individual has never been the customer. The real customer is the person who orders six dozen red pens, one box of folders, and a stapler. The key to success, therefore, is to be able to satisfy that customer. That's where the customer service department becomes so important. The people in that department touch that customer more than anybody.

## EDI AND THE FUTURE OF CUSTOMER SERVICE

The folks in customer service have several functions. We often think of them as simply taking phone orders and providing information about products and order processing. But that's only a small piece of the business—and a piece that's getting smaller as we become more technically capable through the use of electronic data interchange (EDI).

Right now, 60 percent of the business at Staples National Advantage comes in electronically. If you add in the amount that arrives by fax, the total jumps to between 90 and 95 percent. This represents a tremendous growth over just a few years ago. At the beginning of the 1990s, the ratio was probably 50:50. If you go back to the 1980s, you'll find that it was probably 90:10—the other way.

The fax is still a major means of communication in our industry, but not for long. As Internet traffic increases, faxing will practically disappear. Accordingly, from a customer service point of view, taking orders will be the smallest percentage of the job. Customer service representatives in the next few years will be spending increasing amounts of time providing information about products and services. No matter how much information you have on the Internet, no matter how much you offer through media such as catalogs, people will still call up to find out details about product features and availability. Therefore, we will always need to provide a lot of training to ensure that customer service personnel can satisfy our customers' need to know.

Customers expect much more of us today than they did ten or fifteen years ago. I assume that this expectation will move at warp speed in the future. We read a lot about downsizing at major companies. What that means in the area of purchasing is that fewer and fewer people are administrating. So what's expected of us in the customer service area is significantly greater today than ever before, and it will continue to grow exponentially.

Take a company like Prudential Insurance, which had its own purchasing department of sixty or seventy people. If a question about a product arose, company managers would call their own people or check with their own stockroom on the status of deliveries. Now the responsibility has been moved to the vendor, which, in this case, is Staples National Advantage. Those questions now come directly to us.

To complicate matters, the managers asking the questions want a lot more information about products and deliveries than ever before. And at the same time these customers want more information, they also have more questions of a technical nature—which they want answered within an hour or so of when they call. They keep raising the bar, and we have no choice but to learn to jump higher.

In addition, because the customer is placing orders electronically, we at the customer service end have to invest more money in capturing and providing the information they require. In other words, we're investing in individual capital to be able to answer our customers' questions in an intelligent manner. To do that, we need to find the best qualified people we can, train them continuously, and keep up the level of our service.

## CAPITALIZING ON DETAILS

Because our computer system contains a log of every account and every customer who calls in with a complaint or comment, we know the details of the purchases those customers make. We also know about special instructions the customer has for orders and deliveries, special handling, and the like. We plan to develop a data bank full of information as detailed as the kind of fax machine a customer has. That way, when a customer asks for information about ink cartridges and fax paper, we can accomplish some cross-selling at the same time.

When a customer phones, you're handed the perfect opportunity to do some outbound telemarketing. You have the benefit and resource of the customer calling you for information, and you'd be less than smart if you didn't take the time to make the best of that resource. This is one of the many ways in which we try to "know" our customers, to understand what they do and how they do it.

## REDUCING NONPRODUCTIVE CALLS

Because our order entry is done electronically, using either EDI or fax, about 95 percent of our orders come in electronically. Essentially, we receive two kinds of calls: requests for product information and inquiries about an order. Checking on an order does not mean that there is something wrong with the product or the delivery. It simply indicates that somebody is looking for information about an order. But for us, it is a "nonproductive" call.

Of course, a customer service representative still logs in the call, for two main reasons: First, we want to keep track of every call; second, we want to find out if the customer is experiencing a recurring problem. If a group of customers from Ohio call about deliveries, we know we have a problem at the warehouse shipping the orders or at the distribution end, whether it's UPS or a freight carrier. Keeping track of these calls gives us a chance to solve the real problem.

All calls come into our central customer service facility. After logging in the call, we assign each account to two eight-person teams—a primary team and a secondary backup team. The customer will not be connected to a different person each time he or she calls. Our teams are familiar with each account assigned to them and can answer the most specific question. So if a call comes in and all members of the primary team are servicing other customers, the caller will automatically be forwarded to somebody on the secondary team. This ensures that every call is handled by someone familiar with that account, and it results in improved and more efficient customer service.

The sales representatives and the regional vice president meet with the sales team to smooth out potential problems or conflicts, while our service representatives develop a deeper understanding of a customer's needs. If we don't provide exemplary customer service, we will lose that customer. People come to appreciate that somebody at Staples cares about them and treats them as individuals.

For instance, we might receive a call at 8:00 A.M. from a customer who needs a thousand binders by 3:00 P.M. It's a rush job that requires special routing. But our customer service teams are accustomed to dealing with deliveries that are out of the ordinary. One of our people can also locate the order-control number for a shipment, check to see that the order has been processed, and determine exactly where the shipment is and when the customer will receive it.

## THE NEW ROLE FOR CUSTOMER SERVICE

Customers ask for many additional services today. There are special delivery instructions that have to be taken care of. People may have rush orders coming through, so they ask you to stay open at night. They need different order-entry systems. For example, General Mills wants to use an interactive voice response (IVR) system. They may not have computers and PCs at all their locations, but they still want to be connected electronically. So we've created an IVR system that enables the customer to call a toll-free number and then use the telephone as a computer to place an order.

I believe we're soon going to have to face the need for

standardization. In order to save yourself and your customers money and time, you need to develop a standardized system. Today, major corporations expect their vendors—in this case, Staples National Advantage—to come up with systems that meet their needs and save them money. They put the responsibility for creating and developing these systems on our backs. They expect significantly more from us than ever before. In the past, a customer wanted twelve dozen pencils at a competitive price shipped out today. Today, those same customers want us to keep up with their inventories and supply the products they need when they need them. Those requirements are expanding customer service, especially if we at Staples National Advantage hope to remain competitive.

In the long run, therefore, the customer service department will have, perhaps, the lion's share of responsibility in determining which accounts are retained and allowed to grow. We won't have as much impact on the acquiring of accounts (although we'll have some); our major issue will be retaining them. From the point of view of prices, the field of competition is leveling. None of us will have a huge advantage in purchasing; we're all multibillion-dollar companies, and our costs will be approximately the same. The key to competitive advantage will be the quality of service a company offers, and the level of quality will be perceived in the relationships end users experience with the company's customer service department.

Customer service, in short, is one of the main things that distinguishes us from our competitors. In the years to come, customer service will become increasingly more important in distinguishing successful companies from unsuccessful ones. Given our commitment to it, we hope to be ahead of the pack.

■■■

## STAPLES, INC.

### COMPANY PROFILE

| | |
|---|---|
| Business Description | Discount office supply store |
| Website | www.staples.com |
| Founded | 1986 |
| Annual Sales | $3.9 billion |
| Net Income | $106 million |
| Employees | 24,994 |
| Products | Office supply products |
| | Computer hardware and software |
| | Business machines |
| | Office furniture |
| | Business services (printing, copying, binding, computer repair, etc.) |

*Staples is an unusual growth story. In the past seven years, the company's sales have grown seventeen-fold. That's a 54 percent jump each year, a greater pace than even Microsoft (38 percent per year) and Wall Street darling Dell (53 percent) over the same period. To find such a stellar growth rate in an unglamorous industry—selling pens and paper—is even more remarkable when you consider the nature of the business Staples is in.*

*First, Staples operates on paper-thin margins (its net*

*profit isn't even 2.5 percent of sales), which leaves very little room for error or inefficiency. It has no choice but to be fanatic about operations and continuous improvement. It doesn't have the luxury of catering to customer whims the way a Ritz-Carlton does, or to pursue Nordstrom's heroics. (Remember how more than once we heard them say they wanted to meet, not exceed customer expectations? That goes against the popular wisdom spouted in many customer service books and articles.)*

*The second challenge Staples faced in growing so fast was its need to find and train customer service staff (both in the stores and on the phones) to keep up with demand. That's far from a trivial task. Compared with Microsoft, which simply copies its software, or Dell, which cranks up its manufacturing plant to assemble more PCs, Staples is more people-dependent in its customer service operations. (Of course, Microsoft and Dell have their own people challenges—in invention, product development, etc.)*

*The third thing to note is how Staples' marketplace is changing. When the superstore concept was first introduced some dozen years ago, there was a large unmet demand for low-cost stationery products. Today, with so many office supply stores, the game has changed; the challenge now is keeping customers rather than getting them.*

*Put these three conditions (tight margins, people-dependence, and market saturation) together, and it's clear that Staples cannot leave things to chance—it has to have a highly effective process of running its customer service activities. In that sense, it is a more pronounced case of a company that has built and refined a process consisting of four elements useful for anyone who's designing a top-notch service system. That process is an ongoing sequence of:*

- Gaining a better understanding of customer expectations.
- Translating that understanding into operational requirements and performance standards.
- Training employees and encouraging continuous learning.
- Monitoring and tracking outcomes to ensure you stay the course, such as metrics. (Staples' C.A.R.E. program is an example of how the company put this sequence into effect.)

*Readers should pay particularly close attention to the first element: understanding the customer. Staples' practices to develop the personal touch have lots to recommend them:*

*Boost your frontline workers' sensitivity to what customers experience by having workers check out other stores or rival companies. (Have them report back, as did Staples' staff, after trying to return a product without a receipt.) Put your own employees in place as mystery shoppers or mystery customers, so they can see things from another perspective. Encourage them while in this role to look for both great ideas and things that could be improved upon.*

*Encourage and insist on regular role-playing (as Staples does). Your employees need to go through the paces, and* exposing them to some tricky and extraordinary situations will prep them for customer interactions and raise their sensitivity level so they can better deal with emotions such as anger.

Hold up a mirror: Videotaping and subsequent peer "feedback," uncomfortable as they may be, are absolutely great ways to break through blinders, bad habits, and defensive behavior.

Get your managers exposed to their customers' point of view. Replicate Staples' practice of having them call all their top customers at least once a year, work in customer service roles a few times per year, or listen in regularly on customer service calls.

The hallmark of great service operations is their ability to empathize with customers—to see things from the customers' perch, then improve the experiences of those customers without dragging down the service providers' operations. That's the personal touch that I see at Staples.

# 6

# United Services Automobile Association

*Hardwire Service Innovation*

Sometimes great ideas are born out of necessity. The United Services Automobile Association (USAA), one of the world's most successful insurance and financial services companies, was originally founded in San Antonio in 1922 by twenty-five U.S. Army officers who had grown tired of being rejected as "transients" and "bad risks" by one auto insurer after another. Unable to acquire policies through the conventional route because of the physical risks and frequent relocation inherent in their profession, they solved their problem by forming an insurance reciprocal—an association in which they insured each other.

Still headquartered in San Antonio, USAA has a world-wide membership of more than three million strong today. Once open only to active-duty army officers, it has grown to include members from all branches of the military, retired and former military officers, their families, and (most recently) enlisted personnel on active duty and active in the National Guard or Reserve. These changes have led *to increased diversity among members; 95 percent of all active U.S. military officers now have USAA policies, while 10 percent of members have no military experience.*

*The scope of the company has expanded over the past seventy-five years as its numbers have increased. Now a diversified financial services association of fifty-four subsidiaries and affiliates, it offers a wide variety of products and services: property and casualty insurance; life and health insurance; no-load mutual funds; relocation services; a discount brokerage service; a travel agency; a catalog-merchandise service for members; annuities; and the full-service USAA Federal Savings Bank, which is backed by the FDIC.*

*No matter the area being examined, USAA and its almost 18,500 employees draw praise. The company was listed among the nation's top employers in the best-selling book* The 100 Best Companies to Work for in America, *which called it "a safe harbor where employees have incredible opportunities." In its June 1995 issue,* Money *magazine rated the USAA bank as the "Best Bank in America," while* CIO *magazine referred to USAA in August of that same year as one of the top twenty-one consumer-services companies in information technology for "providing the best infrastructures, applications and interfaces, and the training and backup to go with them."*

## BILL COONEY
### President, Property and Casualty Insurance Group

What are the secrets behind our success? For one thing, we've always made customer service our top priority. We have an advantage over other insurance firms because we intimately understand exactly who most of our member-customers are. For more than seventy-five years, we've been dealing with military personnel and their families, and we've grown increasingly sensitive to the life events and issues they must often face—including relocation, disability, and untimely death. What helps in this understanding, of course, is that about 15 percent of USAA employees—myself included—are former military personnel or now serve in the National Guard or Reserve. Many other employees have been exposed to military life through a spouse or parent who was or is in the service. We're sympathetic as a company to the experiences of our members because in many cases we share those same experiences.

At USAA we seek to know our customers. We turn this knowledge into a relationship with the customer, then deepen it by identifying and satisfying additional customer needs. Combining our intimate understanding of members with an innovative use of technology, we are able to maintain service standards even as our membership rapidly increases. The proof is in the numbers: 98 percent of our customer base is in the top two quintiles of customer satisfaction, and 98 percent of our members renew their policies annually.

Our membership trusts us. That's another big key to our success. And when people trust USAA to provide them with a product or service, that makes a major difference in their allegiance to our company. As long as we continue to give our customers what they want when they want it, many of them never consider going anywhere else. They just keep buying from us—period.

How do we build this trust? By providing the type of one-stop service and customer intimacy that people are yearning for today, then continually striving to improve it. When you go to a typical insurance company, you'll find a claims organization, a policy service organization, an underwriting organization, and so on. We're taking out all those stovepipes, those discrete and separate functions, and creating in their place a cross-functional organization. Our goal is to have the customer standing right in the middle of their service team, so he or she has to make only one phone call. There's no pass-off, no transfer. Just one call. We can't do that all the time, but we're heading that way.

We have customers now who won't even talk to someone other than their primary service representative. They just say, "No, that's all right, I don't need to speak to a teammate. I'll just leave a message for Mary Jane, and I know she'll take care of it." Our employees build this level of loyalty because they are passionate about serving people, doing things for them as individuals, not just as nameless customers.

We ask our people to do the right things for the right reasons, regardless of what those reasons happen to be. Our goal is to get everybody to take that attitude. If they have that attitude, they'll do the right thing while they're on the phone with a member. Achieving it is a cultural step. Our customer-oriented culture results from extensive training in correct procedures and customer service techniques. We put significant emphasis on measuring satisfaction and handling complaints. And let's not forget the power of peer pressure—co-workers reminding each other that quality service and meeting the needs of members are our goals.

It's not so much a business thing as it is an emotional thing. I tell people, "If you don't like helping people, don't come to work here. This is not the right place for you. But if you do like helping people—making their lives better, getting them out of bad situations—this is the place to be."

Our people take this thinking to heart. Right now we have seven thousand people out there taking calls from members. And I guarantee you that at least one thousand of those employees are doing something above and beyond the normal realm of customer service to help members out.

The American business community is coming out of the old assembly-line mentality carried over from the manu- facturing plants of the industrial age. We've been working on this for the last five or six years. Like employees at other companies, some of our people grew up with the assembly- line mentality: getting to work at 8:00 in the morning, being monitored all day, taking lunch when the whistle blew, and having the widgets in their baskets counted before they were allowed to leave. As long as you reached your numbers, you were fine.

Well, that's not fine anymore. Now you've got to figure out what you should be doing with your customers out there. Even ten years ago, all our customers wanted was for us to take care of their transactions. "I'll call when I want you to add my car to the policy," they would say, "and you'll do it." That was the deal.

Now the customers need—and want—more. "Wait a minute," they'll say. "When I call you, I want to make sure you take care of my life." It's a different game entirely.

## ECHO—LETTING CUSTOMER VOICES RESONATE

Up until a few years ago, we did the same normal annual surveys that every company does. Then we came to realize they were neither timely enough nor completely useful. How can you run a business when you're not in constant communication with your customers? How can you afford to wait nine or ten months until a customer survey comes back to see how well you're doing? We determined that we had to change. We needed to know what was happening with our membership today—not months down the road. Only then could we guarantee them the best service possible.

Since 1994, USAA service representatives have recorded the views of our membership onto the company's ECHO ("Every Contact Has Opportunity") system. The system takes in about 1,500 customer comments weekly, yet it was very quick to build. It was up and running in about five months. What it has done is focus the entire company on the current needs of our members. At any given time we have seven thousand employees on the phone talking to members, and every one of those employees has the ability to make a real-time input into this system and let the entire staff know what a particular member thinks about us—the good and the bad.

It's actually very simple to use the system. Our customer representatives are all sitting in front of computers already; they just have to key into a special screen, and an ECHO form will automatically be called up. Then they just fill in a few blanks with the member commentary. They can immediately log in what the member has to say or make their own observations on how the member viewed a particular product or service. The entire process takes as little as thirty seconds.

When the representative hits the "send" button, the comments are immediately transmitted to a special unit of "action agents" who work full-time categorizing the comments by subject for the rest of the staff to see. These action agents go over each ECHO issue individually. If it's just a local problem, they'll get it out to the region involved, but if it's a larger issue, they will send it back out to everyone so we can look at it from across the company. When appropriate, action agents also get back to the customers involved to let them know we're acting on their comments.

Because of what we get out of our ECHO system, we are actually changing the way we do business and put together products. I've got a list as long as my arm of changes implemented due to the system. They've included everything from improvements in our communication with members to new products and services, such as special rebates for long-term members, insurance protection for hearing aids, and builder's risk insurance for members constructing new homes. In each case, we try and responded to what members tell us they wished we would do. Changes have included everything from improvements in our member communication to new products and services, such as special rebates for long-term members, insurance protection for hearing aids, and builder's risk insurance for members constructing new homes.

Our representatives may actually fill out only a couple of ECHO forms every few weeks. On the surface that doesn't seem like much, but add them together and we've got several thousand forms coming in weekly from throughout the company. This wealth of membership feedback allows us to study different areas where we may have problems with new offerings. Did we not have the right products? Are the rates too high? Were members not pleased with some of the correspondence we sent them? Did they not understand the policy? Did we not answer the phone quick enough for them? Were they treated badly? There is a whole raft of things to consider, and ECHO offers insight into them very quickly. The system stores everything and allows us to trend and follow feedback over time.

If we send out a letter to members today outlining a change in our homeowner's coverage, for example, I will know almost immediately exactly what members think about the change. Members will call in with their feedback, and our representatives will enter that feedback into the ECHO system. Once the responses are evaluated, we can use them to help in our future decision making. If there is widespread disapproval of the change, we may consider revising or doing away with it. If the responses are predominantly favorable, we may consider more such changes in the future.

Even if a member doesn't make a direct comment, the ECHO system can be helpful. We've got good people, and they can usually recognize what's on the minds of our members. After a customer interaction, a representative might put a write-up into the system that says, "I talked to this member, and although he didn't say it, I know he didn't like XYZ." So although there hasn't been an official complaint made, other agents and management are alerted to a potential problem with a product offering.

Like other companies, we certainly make mistakes from time to time. But as soon as we find out we've done something wrong, we correct it. ECHO tells us right away, and we jump on it. We go in and tear apart the process, all the while saying, "How the heck did this happen?" We don't just try to get rid of the individual member complaint and smooth things over. That doesn't do any good. What we're trying to look for is what caused the complaint in the first place. One of my favorite stories is how we fixed a TelePrompTer problem thanks to ECHO. An older member complained about the system, and we were able to make the fix in hours.

Of course, the disgruntled member hears from us as well. Our employees can immediately send an apologetic gift out to people. You just punch one key, and the next thing you know there is a small gift going out along with a note that essentially says, "I'm sorry. We fouled this up and we'll do better next time." We also try to get back to the member with a phone call somewhere in the first twenty-four to forty-eight hours, then follow the call up with another letter.

This type of real-time response system comes in very handy when we have what I like to call "hot topics." Take, for example, the air-bag issue. It was a big debate in the news recently whether air bags do more harm than good because they deploy so powerfully they can injure or kill small children sitting in the front seat. If I want to know how our members feel about this issue before making any policy changes, I can go out and tell our people, "OK, one of the hot topics I want you to look for today is the air-bag issue. See if you can talk to a couple of people and get their opinions." In two hours, I can potentially get thousands of comments.

Putting ECHO in place was one of the biggest things we've done here in several years. Now we know exactly what's going on with our members. That's a powerful tool.

This new way of dealing with customers is about responsiveness: doing whatever you can to meet their needs. It's about making decisions, getting the help of your co-workers and the people above you, and possessing the freedom to make choices. It's a completely new mind-set, which we encourage in employees by maintaining a working environment that motivates them to provide expert, personalized service others have a tough time matching. We remind employees constantly that their personal involvement in meeting our members' needs and expectations is essential. Their involvement results in service our members deserve, and service we hope cannot be matched by anyone, anywhere.

Once you have the freedom to go the extra mile for customers, it is much easier to deliver the type of dedicated service that results in long-term relationships. Here's a recent example of a situation where we provided great loyalty to our members. A woman in the army was transferred to Fort Sam Houston here in San Antonio. She and her husband drove into town so she could start her training, and right after they got here somebody stole their van with their wallets and all their money in it. Since the wife was in training, the husband didn't know whom to call. So he called us.

The representative taking the call listened as the man told his story. "We just moved into town, my wife is in training, and we have no money," he pleaded. "What do I do?" Our representative didn't hesitate. She got off the phone, drove over to the couple's hotel, picked the man up, and took him to stay at a friend's place temporarily. Then the representative arranged for a church to get involved in further helping the couple. Then she went back to the office to finish her shift.

All in a day's work.

## THINKING FACE-TO-FACE: THE TRAINING COMPONENT

You can talk about great service all day, but the only thing that makes it happen are the people. If you don't have the right culture and the right training programs in place, you can do all the talking you want about quality service but you're not going to get there.

It starts with the hiring process. You've got to have the right testing up front, the right interview process, and then be able to pick the right people who have the talent you need and who believe in and live the customer service ethic. That's number one. You've got to get the right people in the door.

Number two, you have to have a strong training program. This program must embody all the principles of USAA—our reputation, the image we want to maintain, how we want our members treated, and what's acceptable and not acceptable in terms of employee behavior. To get up to speed, our new representatives spend an average of ten full weeks studying everything associated with a customer service position of this type: policy service and claims, USAA customer demographic profiles, telephone technique, conflict resolution, relationship management, complaint handling, satisfaction measurement, and needs analysis.

Participating in what we call "pipeline" training is a full-time occupation for new customer-contact employees. The workers are paid while they attend class, and professionals from our Training and Development Department conduct the training. We measure an employee's success by administering performance-based exercises at various points during a course. The exercises involve simulations of circumstances the worker may encounter during phone contacts with our members. To graduate, our employee-students must maintain at least an 85 average during the training.

New representatives must also have a strong element of technical training, and we include that in the curriculum. So, all told, new employees stay in very concentrated job-related training classes for up to ten weeks. And even when they get to the floor and start making customer calls, these workers are still being monitored and culturalized.

We also have a new system called Automated Coaching and Mentoring that could become the most powerful tool in the training world. A manager using it can observe a representative who is speaking on the phone to a customer and actually see the entire conversation as it is taking place printed out on the representative's PC screen. After the call is over, the manager and employee can look at the transcription and discuss how the interaction went in step-by-step detail. It's great for representatives to see for themselves what they did and didn't ask members. Sometimes what they actually said is far different from what they remember.

## FACE-TO-FACE BY PHONE

People take it as a given when they call USAA that they're going to get their policy when and where they should get it, and that it will cover the things our representative said it would cover. What isn't a given is what we talk about with our customers, and how we talk to them. And that's a key point to the whole transaction.

So we do two things: We make it very easy for employees to "give the givens," and we make sure we also train them to provide the portion of the transaction that's really important. When I talk about really important, I'm referring to the kind of image you get from us. Did we treat you respectfully? Did we treat you in a manner that makes you want to call us back sometime? I've got to produce a policy, and it has to be correct. But the fact is, how I treat you on the phone when you're talking to me is absolutely essential.

It starts with our new member salespeople. We have about three hundred people in place trained specifically to handle new members the first time they call us. We work very hard at making these calls successful. The salespeople are well trained in exactly what it takes to present the image of this company in a way that meets the expectations of customers. They learn that the first phone call is the one that can likely create the full picture of what USAA is all about in the mind of a customer. With this much on the line, everything they say is of key importance.

Our employees working on phones are well trained to gauge during each call the extent to which that member wants to be informed and helped. That's the pitch here. If our people understand this goal we have, this passion for taking care of people, they're going to say the right things.

Think of how you feel yourself when you call someplace and the person who answers treats you well, is courteous and professional, and knows what to do to take care of your needs in one call. What do you normally do when you get off the phone? You probably say to yourself, "That was a pleasant experience. That person helped me out." But when you hear, "We're not sure we can deal with it today, you'll have to call back tomorrow," or, "Yeah, well, we might be able to do it, but I can't promise anything," you get an entirely different feeling. Now you're saying to yourself, "I don't have confidence in these people at all."

So it's the way employees present themselves to each of our members that counts. Even though we're often on the phone with our members, we try to make them feel just like we're face-to-face with them. That's the key. Some people will tell you that actually being face-to-face is always better. But then members have to drive somewhere, or be inconvenienced by having somebody come to their house. If we can provide the same level of service and intimacy by phone, we're actually intruding on our members far less.

## BACK TO SCHOOL
We devote a large amount of in-house resources to helping employees with self-development and the enhancement of their leadership and organizational skills. On top of his or her initial training, the average USAA employee gets more than sixty-five hours of annual job-specific and generic instruction. The company also offers about two hundred different no-cost courses on subjects including benchmarking, process improvement techniques, team building, and facilitation that we conduct in our seventy-five on-campus classrooms. There is no requirement that our people participate, but employees are usually interested in developing their skills—and as a result the courses are very popular.

One course we offer focuses on one-to-one communication and the secrets to positive face-to-face and telephonic interaction. The importance of such skills cannot be overemphasized when you consider that we do most our business with members by phone. Another four-hour coaching course focuses on giving leaders and managers skills they can use to improve employee performance—and, consequently, our service delivery—through effective coaching. We also have self-help resource centers open twenty-four hours a day, seven days a week, where employees can study a variety of subjects at their own pace while off-duty. Computer software is available at these centers for employees to develop math, writing, and reading skills, and there are self-help courses to help people work on self-improvement or prepare for college-entrance exams.

After getting feedback from workers, we realized that besides these on-site measures we needed to enact additional changes in order to build the caring, nurturing environment we were after. So we got in touch with Darden Business School at the University of Virginia and created a one-week executive management course there especially for USAA leadership. It cost us several million dollars and took a big commitment on our part. But it was worth it.

We designed the course in the spring of 1996, and our first class of thirty USAA managers attended in the spring of that year. Since then, we've sent every manager we have through the Darden course—all 1,250 of them. Some had never been to college before, let alone to an executive management course at a top institution. They lived on the UVA campus for a week, working in a high-energy atmosphere where things were going on day and night. And they gave the course such rave reviews it was unbelievable. Managers were shaking their heads, just saying, "Wow, great stuff." And it was all undertaken because of employee feedback.

The course has three major segments. The first is a strategic thinking and leadership block in which students examine case studies of successful companies that despite being in other industries draw parallels with USAA. This is followed by a business-simulation segment that includes a very detailed model of the property and casualty insurance business and is designed to develop business acumen. Personal leadership is our third block; it revolves around case studies and discussion of leadership principles. The bottom line at Darden—our goal for the course—is to foster better leadership, then use it to improve our performance in delivering the highest quality of service possible to our members.

## STRUCTURE SET FOR SERVICE

Innovation is a major factor in our ability to develop strong bonds with widely dispersed customers. From the start, our relationships with clients have been indirect—established primarily through mail and phone. We were quick to see the competitive advantage that information technology could offer in enhancing these interactions, and we were pioneers in the use of computers to automate insurance records and underwriting data.

We began using what was then called electronic data processing in the late 1950s, installing some of the first computers to be used in a commercial environment. Our early applications were in policy issue, accounts receivable, and direct-mail marketing. Today all our customer service representatives are linked into one of the nation's most advanced computer-driven customer information systems. In 1969 it took fifty-five steps and up to six weeks to issue and deliver a USAA insurance policy; a policy can now be issued in one day—and delivered overnight.

We maintain an extensive database on all our member-customers, including full demographic data and documentation on all the USAA products and services they have previously used. Each interaction between a representative and member is recorded into the database, where it becomes a "living document" immediately available to all other representatives to help in future interactions with that same member.

USAA's Image System, the largest system of its kind in the world, contains electronic copies of every "paperwork" item we have ever compiled on a customer. The system can scan forty thousand pages of mail each day, allowing for their instant access by a policy service representative at over 11, 700 Image computer terminals across the United States.

Simply put, everything our reps need to know about every USAA member is always at their fingertips. Because we have so much information to bring to each conversation, we are able to successfully handle 86 percent of member requests on first contact. And this is one reason why our customer-service retention is about 98 percent—and why half those who do leave eventually return. That's a retention rate most insurers cannot match.

## CREATIVE AND COLLECTIVE EXCELLENCE

In the factories of old, workers simply followed the foreman's orders, met their guidelines, and that was it. We didn't just want our 18,500 employees acting as order takers doing what management told them. We wanted to tap into their creativity, to see them responding to the business world and doing the right things for each member they interacted with.

We're always hoping and looking to create a structure where leadership, empowerment, creativity, and change make a difference. One that members don't worry about, and where employees—and this is the key—are motivated to provide personalized service that can't be matched by anyone else. When I say anyone, I'm not just talking about other insurance companies. I'm talking about anyone, anywhere.

This environment we envisioned was a place where everybody has the opportunity to do their very best—and have a good time doing it. A place that actually encourages change and creativity, not one that stifles it. A place that produces satisfied workers, who in turn provide customer-driven service delivery that's flexible and ever-improving.

This is where the PRIDE (for Professionalism Results in Dedication to Excellence) system comes in. We started the PRIDE program in 1990 to promote teamwork and innovation for improved productivity and service. It encourages the active participation of frontline employees in identifying problems, forming action teams, and learning advanced problem-solving skills. Employees who participate also learn action-planning skills and how to plan and execute change initiatives. A critical element of the process is two-way communication. You cannot downplay its importance. We have all learned there must be communication going in every direction—from management to employee, from employee to management, and from peer to peer. This is vital to our success.

Can a team take action on its own? It depends. A unit team can decide to program the unit's keyboards to facilitate interaction with members while avoiding expensive system changes. If a team recommendation has broader impact, management gets involved. Our business-casual dress policy and on-site day-care initiatives started as ideas that were surfaced by our PRIDE teams over an extended period. Senior management got involved, and the result was a global corporate solution.

There are now hundreds of PRIDE teams in place, and, in effect, one big PRIDE team encompassing all of us. Members of these teams try to figure out better ways of doing things. A team in our After-Hours Policy Service area is an excellent example. It spearheaded the development of templates for use in our on-line documentation system. The templates have preformatted information in them normally found on paper applications, forms, and checklists. Using the templates reduces the time spent keying data and lets us reinvest that time in providing members with more thorough information on their insurance coverages.

When it's done, a team may come to brief me on its new ideas, and I can decide whether to go with them. The process is very quick, and it's gotten employees involved with helping us solve problems head-on.

We came out with ten PRIDE principles that all our employees know and are expected to live by:

> Exceed customer expectations.
> Live the Golden Rule.
> Be a leader.
> Participate and contribute.
> Pursue excellence.
> Work as a team.
> Share knowledge.
> Keep it simple.
> Listen and communicate.
> Have fun.

If you're not living by this credo, you should figure out what's stopping you and change it.

When we first put this environment in place seven years ago, we knew we were going to have to change our service delivery model to meet the new twenty-first-century requirements of the customer. The PRIDE component, in effect, has created an environment where it's easier to change. And believe me, changing thousands of people overnight is not easy. But it's worth it.

## PUTTING PRIDE TO WORK

You can spot it in a heartbeat if employees on the phone take pride in their work. All you've got to do is listen. A few years ago we received a phone call that I happened to be monitoring. An eighty-one-year-old lady from California called in and got a young service rep on the line. The service rep taking the call was about twenty-four years old.

This woman said to our young service rep, "I need some help—but I'm not sure what I need." She began rambling. The service rep, who's used to getting things moving, was trying to manage this sensitively. Finally this eighty-one-year-old woman said, "I'm sorry that I sound disjointed, but I just lost my husband three weeks ago and I don't know what to do." Without missing a lick, the rep said, "Please accept our condolences, we're really sorry. I'd like to help you. What is it that I can do to assist you?"

"Well," she replied. "I've got all these papers in my hand, but I know some more are scattered all over the place. I know he had some life insurance policies, and I know I've got automobile insurance. I just don't know what to do about them." The service rep then said, "Why don't you go and try to find all the papers, and I'll wait." The woman warned that it might take her a long time, but the rep said she would wait.

It did take her a long time, but the woman eventually came back on the line with all her paperwork in hand. An hour and five minutes later, when the call finally ended, the young rep had taken care of all of the woman's problems including her life, estate, and car insurance. The average call in those days was about 4.9 minutes. The woman said to the rep, "I just want to tell you this is the nicest thing that's happened to me in three weeks." Then she sent the rep flowers.

Those are the kinds of things that go on every day. We have members who send our people flowers on a regular basis when they provide this kind of service. It goes back to our original philosophy. If you have a passion for helping people, it really helps. If you only have a passion for selling policies, that's a problem. Our reps have no quotas for phone calls or time limits on calls they handle. They spend the time required to take care of members' needs, whatever that time may be.

## VIRTUAL TEAMING: GETTING HELP WHEN IT'S NEEDED

If a customer calls in with a request that an insurance representative can't handle, our system is set up so that all the rep has to do is bring another person up on the line who can take care of those special needs.

In some cases, this other person may not even be a USAA employee. There are some products—for instance, aircraft—that we don't normally write insurance for. But since four thousand of our members have airplanes, we still offer the coverage. We have a general agency that partners with appropriate companies, and a USAA representative can just call up a buddy in the general agency and say, "I've got an aircraft insurance policy on the line, can you handle it for me?" The next thing you know the rep at our general agency is on with the customer working the aircraft policy.

By partnering up with another carrier, we maintain customer trust; the customers get the expertise and help they need, but they also know that we're involved and ultimately responsible for the service they receive.

## GETTING MANAGEMENT'S EAR

Our on-line documentation system (ODOC-E) is in a sense an ECHO system for employees. It gives employees a chance to do the exact same thing themselves that they're helping members do with ECHO—provide feedback to management on how they feel things are running. An employee may just write something down like, "If you can get me a better Image system, I can do this job faster." It could even be as simple as "Why didn't you guys give us the day after Christmas off?" It's almost like an electronic suggestion system. Suggestions go to action agents; these agents determine what, if anything, we can do with the idea.

We never run out of ideas. I've had a couple cross my desk recently that were especially useful. One ODOC-E letter said some supervisors were penalizing employees in performance reports for using their sick leave or occasionally coming to work late. We took a look into that, and as a result we're now going to make sure we always give fair and proper consideration to absences and tardiness that occur for reasons beyond a person's control—such as family illness or transportation problems. Another letter suggested we offer on-site training for employees who want to learn to use a personal computer at home. Comments like these from employees can alert upper management to a problem causing tension within a department. Resolving such problems improves the work environment and the quality of service we give to members.

## THIS IS YOUR LIFE

We try to know what "life events" we're dealing with for each of our customers so we can maximize the amount of assistance we offer them. Say Customer X is thinking about buying a home, and he calls in wanting to know what kind of insurance would best suit him. We can just give him an answer, of course, but we also now have the opportunity to help him in other areas. Maybe he don't have the home yet and is wondering how much it will cost. We can plug into our bank on the spot and check for very low mortgage rates. If he needs part or all of the house inspected, we can help him with that.

In addition, we also have a Home Help Line that allows members in the United States, especially those members with home-owner policies, to call an 800 number and get answers to problems from a network of on-site tradespeople and experts. For example, we have many elderly widows in our company who have been members for forty-five years, and when they run into a crisis they'll just call up and say, "I don't know an electrician in town," or "I've got a leaky faucet." In the course of a phone call, we've actually helped people change their kitchen faucets.

We were the ones who created this type of service in the

United States, and we believe we're still the only insurance company offering it. It's especially helpful when you deal with customers like ours who are constantly moving. Every time they come into a new city, they'll invariably call us up and say, "I don't know who to get to come fix up my house." Our staff can either help the customers take initial steps themselves or provide the number of an appropriate tradesperson or expert to call. Our members trust our recommendations, and that trust translates into long-term customer loyalty.

We categorize our membership into different customer groups. We know, for example, what likely events a particular group is going to have in the future. If a member is twenty-eight years old and has just been married, we know he or she is probably going to have a child pretty soon. We'll make sure we keep track of the children as they're born, and in time the family will be eligible for X amount of products or services. If a customer calls in and it happens to be the day of his son's birthday, our rep might mention it. We have all the information—kids, parents, cars, homes—right there on the policy.

It's not just growing families that get special treatment. We also know when we have soldiers calling in from overseas and take special measures to give them quicker attention. And because the mail doesn't run as well overseas, we realized a while back that our normal time frame for collecting bills and issuing nonpayment cancellation notices doesn't work for those members working or living abroad. Since they don't get our bills when everybody else does, we've instituted a procedure whereby people overseas have an additional thirty days in which to pay their bill before we take action.

Members who have experienced the death of someone in their family are given their own level of special consideration. "Survivor Teams" have been created inside the company, which alert all necessary USAA representatives of deaths so that members who are in mourning will not be bothered with form notices and unimportant phone calls. Even if this type of customer service goes unnoticed by those it is meant to help, it is no less important.

## Ideas for the Taking

If we can find a good idea somewhere and apply it to this business, we do. You can also learn a lot about what not to do by studying other industries, as well as benchmarking other firms. Our benchmarking partners have included companies such as AT&T, Texas Instruments, Allstate, and CitiCorp. Trends are one thing we pick up on from other companies. We know, for example, that one-stop shopping is great. Our members tell us that. In fact, we get a lot of feedback from our membership. By dealing with the demands of our members, we can establish a sense of where other companies are succeeding and struggling. Most members don't want to stay on the line too long. They want someone to take their problem and run with it. They don't want to have to tell their problem to too many people. They want a quick response. And they don't want it tomorrow, they want it today.

Customers can be very demanding, and we live to meet their demands. They expect the best, so the pressure is on us to give them the best. That's why every day we have to keep looking at how we can do something better tomorrow than we did yesterday.

## GIVING CUSTOMERS WHAT THEY WANT

In 1983, after discovering our members disliked the inconvenience of making claims for personal property, waiting for their claim to be paid, and then shopping for replacement items, we offered them the choice of getting replacement items directly from us instead of retailers. Combined with a new partnership we made with Federal Express at the same time, this service helped reduce the time needed to replace property from three weeks to three days for 95 percent of all items.

As this service grew, our three million members gave USAA the purchasing power needed to negotiate favorable pricing on goods and services. For example, our ability to replace "like and quality" merchandise below retail prices resulted in USAA and participating members saving about $17.4 million in 1996 alone. Later, we began allowing members who had not incurred an insurance loss to use our buying service via catalog sales. These sales leverage acquisition volumes, giving USAA more status in the marketplace. USAA now sells merchandise, jewelry, discounted communication services, cruise travel, rental car discounts, emergency road assistance, computers, and giftware.

When you look at USAA and its various lines of business as a single entity, you see the largest mail-order company in the United States, despite our having no sales force. Taking care of our members' insurance and financial services needs means our employees handle about four hundred thousand voice calls and more than sixteen million computer transactions per day. Despite such demands, we strive to give all our member-customers the feeling that their needs as individuals are being met.

## WHAT'S DOWN THE ROAD?

We're opening up eligibility to enlisted personnel in all fifty states by the end of 1998. That's going very well. Better than we expected, as a matter of fact. Our problem will be how we manage the growth, not the growth itself. That's a nice problem to have. It may take a few years, but we'll definitely double our membership sooner rather than later. We have a tremendous pent-up demand out there.

We just want to be sure that we grow the right way. What we're not going to do under any circumstances is lower the level of service that we've offered over the years to our present membership. To keep your commitment to your current membership, you've got to watch your growth. No matter what, your service should not suffer.

It's really a capacity control issue we're facing. We're bringing a significant number of new customers in, but we need to be very careful. Getting them on the books is not as important to us as it is to provide them with exceptional service once they're on the books.

What we're working on now is similar to what Jack

Welch at General Electric has talked about many times. We want to make sure no matter how big we get that the members still feel that we're a small company that can't wait to do business with them. By the time we get all our technology in place in another couple years, we will be in a position where we can elevate our service to a whole new level of excellence and totally distinguish ourselves from the competition.

Members will feel that they have their own personal team of experts tending to their needs.

Attention and time will be the great differentiators in the new economy, separating the winners from the losers. In true USAA style, we intend to be at the fore of this movement and to excel at both, making our employees and most especially our members both satisfied and proud.

■■■

## UNITED SERVICES AUTOMOBILE ASSOCIATION

## COMPANY PROFILE

| | |
|---|---|
| Business Description | Insurance and financial services |
| Website | www.usaa.com |
| Founded | 1922 |
| Annual Sales | $6.8 billion |
| Net Income | $855 million |
| Employees | 18,500 |
| Products | Property and casualty insurance |
| | Life and health insurance |
| | Annuities |

No-load mutual funds
Real estate opportunities
Discount brokerage service
Banking services

*The comment that struck me most in my interview with General Cooney was that out of the seven thousand people at his company taking calls from customers, one thousand are doing something above and beyond the norm. While I'm sure General Cooney never took an actual head count, his statement speaks volumes about the pride he has in his people—and his expectations for them. "Doing what's expected isn't enough: We need to do things better and better" is what I heard throughout the discussion.*

*Over the years, I have come to know USAA as the kind of organization that has hardwired service innovation into its processes and people. Take a look at its ECHO system, and how it takes USAA well beyond traditional practices. "Every Contact Has Opportunity" is the motto; a gigantic idea-generating machine is the implementation; ongoing innovation is the outcome; and a 2 percent customer attrition rate—versus 15 percent for similar companies elsewhere—is the payoff.*

*Wouldn't you want to put this kind of system high on your wish list of things to do to improve your customer service operations?*

*Before you rush into adopting this approach, however, recognize that its implementation isn't a no-brainer, irre-*

*spective of how easy it appeared for USAA to do. A system like ECHO—and all the other service innovations that were mentioned—must have had their naysayers. To get such newfangled ideas accepted at your organization, consider doing the following:*

- Instead of conducting annual market research surveys that produce quantitative summaries of what customers want, follow the philosophy of relying more heavily on qualitative input from many (in USAA's case, thousands) of individuals—one at a time. Then prepare your market research people and management for a dramatic change from hard numbers and data to soft suggestions and impressions.

- Instead of taking the time to ponder new ideas and submitting them to analytical scrutiny, turn up the heat—using "action agents" (what a great title) to process ideas and suggestions instantly—in real time But before doing so, ask yourself some tough questions. Are your people ready for this? How will management regard such experimentation and its inherent risks? How do you reassure your service staff that they won't end up with a lot of wacky follow-ups that make jobs harder rather than easier? How do you get the organization to accept the inevitable mistakes and mishaps that will occur?

*In many ways, USAA's service innovations remind me of what I've come across in the high-tech industries, which are far removed from insurance and banking. When I think of ECHO, it reminds me of a Silicon Valley notion where ideas get rapidly turned into prototypes that are let loose on the market labeled "beta versions." The customers of these beta products are used to such experimenting. They know there will be bugs and errors to clean up later in the next release/version of the product. Doing the same thing in a business such as insurance seems at first quite a stretch, yet that's what ECHO is all about. It's USAA's equivalent of road-testing its service innovations—a process by which the company and its customers jointly design and refine ways of doing business.*

*Clearly, service innovations such as ECHO, ODOC-E and USAA's radical I/T improvements succeed only because the company nurtures an openness to new approaches. Sending all its managers to the University of Virginia for an in-depth course fits in nicely. Empowering employees at all levels is another manifestation. So ultimately, service innovation requires a receptive environment that stimulates and prods employees to "go above and beyond the norm." It takes an outlook whereby each individual is constantly searching for new and better ways to do things. And what makes this so potent at USAA is that this proactive stance—this desire and commitment to learn and improve—extends to the customer.*

*USAA is taking responsibility for its customers' broader*

*financial needs. It anticipates changes in life events, then suggests and nudges customers into appropriate directions to deal with those needs. And it goes beyond offering just its financial services by embellishing them with auxiliary offerings that round out the overall experience of the customer.*

# About the Editor

Fred Wiersema is a business strategist and sought-after lecturer whose action-provoking insights have inspired companies around the world to sharpen their customer focus, foster a growth culture, and exploit leading-edge practices and technology. He is the founder of Ibex Partners, a think tank on market leadership.

With Michael Treacy, he authored the runaway bestseller *The Discipline of Market Leaders* (1995). The book urges companies to deliver superior customer value through operational excellence, customer intimacy, or product leadership. It appeared on U.S. best-seller lists for nineteen months (including five months as the number one business book) and was translated into sixteen languages. In his follow-up book, *Customer Intimacy* (1996), Wiersema dissects the practices of companies that thrive on close connections with selected customers. With Rosabeth Moss Kanter and John

Kao, he coedited *Innovation* (1997), the first book in the HarperBusiness BusinessMasters series.

Previously, Wiersema was a senior partner and founder of the market leadership practice at CSC Index, the international management consultancy. He has worked with high-profile companies on issues ranging from business development and market strategy to competitive strategy and management alignment. Earlier in his career, he was a business school professor and high-tech executive.

Dr. Wiersema was born in the Netherlands. He holds a doctorate in business administration from Harvard Business School, a master's in marketing from the University of Lancaster, England, and a bachelor's degree in economics from Erasmus Universiteit, Rotterdam. He and his family live in the Boston area.

For thoughts and comments about this book, he can be contacted by fax (781-894-1740) or E-mail (fdw@wiersema.com).

# Index